I0532360

Not My Monkeys

Influencing Without Power

CJ Corki

CJ Corki Publishing LLC
Lakewood, OH

CJ Corki/CJ Corki Publishing
132a Veterans Lane Suite #342
Doylestown, PA/18901
author@cjcorki.com

Publisher's Note: This is a work of fiction. Names, characters, places, and incidents are a product of the author's imagination or personal experiences. Locales and public names are sometimes used for atmospheric purposes. Any resemblance to actual people, living or dead, to businesses, companies, events, institutions, or locales is completely coincidental.

Neither the author nor the publisher assumes any responsibility or liability whatsoever on behalf of the consumer or reader of this material. Any perceived slight of any individual or organization is purely unintentional.

The resources in this book are provided for informational purposes only and should not be used to replace the specialized training and professional judgment of a health care or mental health care professional.

Book Cover Design 2023 100 Covers
Font: OpenDyslexic

Not My Monkeys/ CJ Corki- 1st ed.
ISBN 979-8-9861397-7-7 - Paperback
ISBN 979-8-9861397-8-4 - Hardcover

Na zdrowie to Carl and Generose Szostak, our amazing parents, who conducted their juggling acts center ring as a guide for us on grandparenting and parenting. This book is a tribute to their selflessness and love, and we couldn't be more grateful for their unwavering support. Let's all give a round of applause to the best grandparents and parents under the Big Top!

TABLE OF CONTENTS

Not My Monkeys

Introduction

If the same old-fashioned parenting advice isn't cutting it anymore, let this book guide you to a closer connection.

"The world is changing. We must change with it."
- P.T. Barnum.

As we sit in our bunny slippers, surrounded by the grandchildren's laughter, we are reminded of the countless tales our parents, as grandparents, told over the years. From the quests of fairies to the blooming marshmallow bush, each story has been a window into a magical world filled with wonder and excitement. And as we shared those tales with our grandchildren, we've come to understand the true power of storytelling, a gift we can pass down from generation to generation. As P.T. Barnum says, storytelling allows you to dream with your eyes wide open. It is a unique ability to captivate and transport our audience to a different time and place.

In this book, we invite you to join us on a journey through the art of storytelling, as seen through the eyes of proud grandparents who are honing their craft. We'll dive into how generation gaps can impact relationships and show you practical strategies that will help strengthen bonds.

To equip you with the methods to create and share your unique family history and special abilities, we have created The Intentional Grandparents Series. Using the foundation of the Polish Proverb: Not My Circus, Not My Monkeys, the Series is designed to share how we can raise our ability to shape and strengthen our grandchildren's lives through our values and guidance without the usual power that comes with the parent role. This role should always be considered.

You are no longer in the center ring; your super strength is INFLUENCE.

In this first book, Not My Monkeys, we use humor, wit, and wisdom that outlines the roadblocks and obstacles grandparents face. Every chapter is tailored towards strengthening relationships between wise elders and curious young ones.

By sharing enchanting stories, we provide insight throughout the chapters, and at the end of each chapter, we summarize Fun Things to Do to build those bonds.

1.   TALK – There is no better way to do this than having a good adult-to-adult chat with your own children. Ideas will be provided to add a little bit of fun and insight to the topic of conversation.

2.   RECOMMENDED READING – What a fantastic way to spend time with your grandkids by reading age-appropriate books together! Not only can this be a fun bonding experience, but you can also reinforce positive lessons from the chapter.

3.   QUESTIONS   –   Thought-provoking discussions can spice up a conversation! Whether you're trying to build trust or get the creative juices flowing, using thoughtful questions will show you genuinely care about the discussion.

Wrapping up the chapter is a journal page to record your activity. On the top of the page is the chapter's Core Value. Reflect, record, and regroup on how these relate to the lessons you want to share.

Thank you for joining us under the big top for the main event, Life.

Chapter 1

"The best parents get promoted to grandparents." — Unknown

Who Am I Now?

Where is My Job Description?

I've worked in information technology, finance, human resources, and even customer service, I have had job titles from the mundane to the most powerful. Now, with no job posting, a new role has been thrust upon me. What are the job duties? Somewhere there should be a grandparent job description template, duties, and responsibilities or at least an administrative assistant to support me along the way.

I know I had 9 months to prepare for the role. Now I find that as I speak to other family members in this same grandparent or great grandparent position, the day-to-day job specifications are each unique in their own way. What specific skills do I need to make the transition? What am I supposed to "do"? With every new role I had throughout my career there was a clear written job description, and that description included clearly defined roles, expectations, and goals.

When my first grandbaby, Lucas was born, no one handed me the grandparent manual. My mother and grandmothers were no longer with me, so I searched out other relatives only to find out that there isn't one. Hmmm, I guess writing a job description just might be the start of a book idea...but I digress. Since there is no "how-to" book that I can find that tells me what my job is or even if there is a job, I've moved into foreign territory for someone that has always knew the expectations.

So, new grandparents out there, or veteran grandparents, how did you define your job?

While I wait for your responses, I started to formulate my plans and decided that this new role was going to give me a personal re-boot. What is the role I want to take on? Oh, and did I mention my grandbaby is 3000 miles away? How do I accomplish this with that distance?

Before I present my personal vision of my job to my son and daughter-in-law, I figured I needed to come up with a skeleton of details, so we had a starting point for discussion. You are probably asking why a discussion point with the kids? Well, as I see it, they are my partner in this journey and with their alignment they can help make the plan a reality. After all, who is interacting with the grandkid every day? Who is it that can orchestrate get togethers, phone calls, activities, and stories?

I don't know if my grandparents had a plan, but each side of the family had different interactions with me when I was a kid. My mom's parents lived near our home, and the family business was attached to their home. I saw them every day while working at the store, eating meals in the kitchen, making Easter baskets in the basement. They were truly an extension of my home life and a defining part of my childhood. As for my dad's side of the family my memories are less vivid. There was the yearly Christmas Eve party when all the cousins, uncles and aunts would get together, but other than that there was a periodic visit to their home, no memories of them coming to ours. Same community, all about the same distance away, yet significantly different interaction.

So, my first decision was easy, yep, Lucas will be in my life. My starting point which was easily accepted was a weekly phone call during the early years, so he can see pictures, start hearing my name and monthly cards that his parents can read to him and ultimately will be our personal communication.

My thoughts about the cards is that it wouldn't just be the "hi, miss you" kind of card but rather something that tells a story. A monthly story of stories from my past, his grandfather's past that he never met, events, traditions or maybe even a defining moment in history, a story of his dad from the past. Something that will give him some insight into the legacy that he will now join.

I am guessing that this job description with be morphing over time.

Me...a Grandparent?

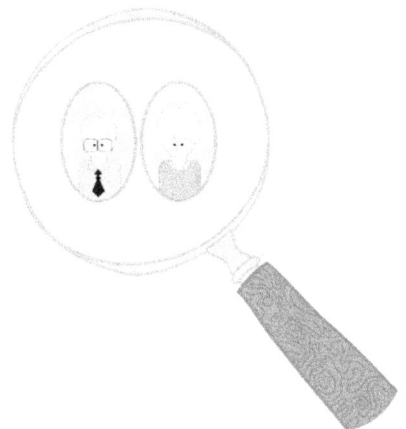

Wow! When did that happen? It can't be me...
...grandparents are old, gray hair wrapped into
a tight bun, wrinkly smiles and when visiting
there was always the smell of something
yummy wafting from the kitchen.

I never "got the memo" on grandparenting, I
don't have gray hair, never wore it in a bun
and as for baking, let along cooking, the only
thing wafting from my kitchen is still smell
of something recently burnt.

As I reflect, I was a multi-tasking working
parent, managing family, career, activities and
trying to find a free minute to myself. Today,
I officially became a grandparent. Where did
the time go?

So, the time did fly and there are defining
moments that start today, with the
introduction of this new addition...my first
grandchild.

What does he call me? When I was growing up, the answer was the traditional view. There was my grandma and grandpa, the parents of my mom. On my dad's side there was Grandpa Frank and Bushi (the polish word for grandma).

Easy, I could probably grab one of those, or one might think so, but unfortunately no. There are now step grandparents, divorced grandparents, regular grandparents on both sides of the family. Of course, vying for a name that the others in the extended were personally familiar with made it a race to grabbing the coveted name that will be remembered for generations to come.

The core grandparents grab the coveted Grandma Charlotte and Rosie, another grandma? I think not. Since I am the step grandparent, Grandma Carlene just had more baggage then was worth debating, so the selection for me wasn't going to be as easy.

So, I looked beyond the traditional. What did my parents call themselves? Was it a conscious decision? I find out the answer was a definitive yes! My mom grew up with the Shirley Temple movies (google search her before she was a UN Ambassador) and Heidi being her favorite movie. She decided that the caring, powerful and protective Grandfather from the movie would be my dad's name and hers Grandmother. As the daughter with the first grandchild, I voiced a mild concern that those names might be a mouthful for a young child.

Lesson #1, kids are a sieve and learn whatever you want to teach them. Want to be called Grandmother? No problem, just say it often, refer to yourself as such and the name will stick. Now 30 years later, when discussing my parents, Grandmother and Grandfather rolls trippingly off the tongue of all the grandkids. Mom, you were very wise.

So, back to my dilemma? I needed a name. Some of the names that made the short list were Oma and Opa, German for grandparents, but not being German took that quickly off the list, heading down the language route, Grand mere & Grand pere was viewed and dropped, there was Baba & Gigi, Nana & Papa, MeMaw and Pawpaw. Ugh.

Taking a step back, I looked at my relationship with my stepson, who I knew since he was 5 years old. Not being able to call me Mom while growing up, which felt wrong on so many levels, he and I came up with our own personal term of endearment. He is known by all as Michael or Mike, but "Mi" to me, and no one else, and I became "Car," a shorten version of my name, Carlene.

The decision was clear, expand our personal term of endearment to represent me, Lucas' grandmother is now and forever called, Carma.

My grandson is only 7 months old, but Carma is going to share the story, so Lucas not only continues to call me Carma but understands the why so that he can play it forward for generations to come. What do you want to be called? Or what are some memorable grandparents' names you have heard?

How Not to be a Toxic Grandparent

News alert! I was not a perfect parent! And guess what? There is no such thing as a perfect grandparent either!

I know, I know, that's shocking, but if we are going to take our role as intentional grandparents seriously, then we also must be confident and courageous enough to take our blinders off. Now, if you are like me, it has been a few years since we were actively parenting, and our memory is probably a little vague. At least mine is. But if we genuinely self-assess and then finally accept that we were not perfect in that role, we can design our new role and intent with our grandchildren.

It's normal for grandparents to want to spoil their grandkids, or maybe meddle, a little, but it comes from love — usually.

So how do you go from caring, loving grandparent to toxic? Let's start with the definition of toxic. Merriam-Webster's definition of toxic is "very harmful or unpleasant in a pervasive or insidious way." So, taking that definition a step farther, I would add the grandparent component to the definition and include in toxic, a lack of empathy for other people's feelings...especially your children.

Yes, I will repeat it, we were NOT perfect parents. If we hang on to that belief of perfection, and it is not held in check, we can quickly become a toxic grandparent.

Now I believe that most of us can differentiate between being a positive, reinforcing, and supportive grandparent and being the actual parent.

Think back. You remember those decisions, big or small, that belong solely to you, as the parent. Now, I am not saying that as a grandparent, you don't have opinions. After all, we have lived, and with that living comes to some thoughts, experiences, and best practices. These thoughts, however, could easily be presented as facts. You know those opinions; daycare ideas, food choices, how the child should be disciplined, allowance, bedtime, the list goes on and on.

I have one FACT for you: We don't have the final say on anything that our kids and their spouses, as the parent to your grandchildren, have.

So, what are the signs of a toxic relationship? Well, here are three things can we do that will keep the toxic grandparent devil at bay?

1. Don't insert yourself into the day-to-day activities or decisions being made by the parents. If you have the luxury of living close by and often see your grandchild, you may have an unintended opportunity to watch their decision-making firsthand. It is our job to "speak when spoken to." Don't proactively share how "they should do something." Or worse yet, use guilt, "that's what I did when you were a baby, and look how you turned out."

2. Don't compete with the other grandparents. I do not have the luxury of living close to my grandbaby. The grandparent with day-to-day interaction has proximity and more time with the grandchild. My response to you is, "Get over it."

   This is not a competition. When you have a chance to interact with your grandkids, don't say anything demeaning or harmful about the other party. Acting jealous or hurt does nothing to endear you to the parents or the kids. Find creative ways to have a virtual relationship. Remember, the post office can also be your friend.

3. Don't always be the grandparent baring gifts. It's normal that we want to spoil our grandkids and bring expensive gifts every time we see them. You might think it's ok to provide an overabundance of gifts to outshine the other grandparents or even Santa during the holiday. Oh, and by the way, there are no iPhones, iPods, Gameboys, or PlayStations without

early discussion with the parents. Why? Spoiling the child for a short-term gain for you elevates you to the verge of toxicity.

The intentional grandparent's role is not to challenge the new culture but instead find a new way to fit in. So, take a breath, outline how you would like to fit into their lives, and then have an open and honest discussion with the decision-makers.

Leaning into discomfort will create a new culture that is a win-win for both....and the only winner will be the grandbabies. So, breathe and know that you and the new parents are not perfect, and that's ok.

Re-invent Yourself

You are never too old to reinvent yourself!

After 75 years of living a selflessly devoted, emotionally draining, and yet exhilarating role of being a grandmother, mother, and daughter, one woman set out to lean into discomfort and tackle a new way of communicating with her family, friends, and daughters daily.

Being raised in the era of talking over the fence with neighbors and friends was an everyday occurrence. For the few that lived farther away, snail mail was the most cost-effective form of communication. A postage stamp cost $0.03, and a long-distance phone call was a luxury saved only for emergencies.

While raising her family, juggling multiple responsibilities of work, spouse, and parents, all vying for time and attention, she was no different than any parent during the first 25 years of marriage. The world moved from party lines to princess telephones to car phones to smartphones.

Also, during this time, the world suddenly got smaller. The close loved ones were no longer just a quick walk out to the backyard or down the block for conversations and friendship but were now spread around the country with hundreds of miles and often multiple time zones away.

As John Lennon once said, "Life is what happens to you while you're busy making other plans." This poignant and relevant statement was true "back in the day" and will continue for generations. Numerous famous quotes remind us of time passing. Albert Einstein said, "Time flies when you are having fun," and Ben Franklin said, "Lost time is never found again." The quotes have the same theme, from famous, infamous, or just average people over the days, decades, and centuries.

Time is over in the blink of an eye. As we all move through time, each of us is reinventing ourselves, and sometimes we do it with conscious thought, sometimes not. As this solitary woman decided, today they were going to be with conscious thought.

She was at a pinnacle point in her re-invention. Yes, she has been reinventing herself countless times as the situations arose. Naturally, losing a loved one, parent, or spouse, the change before your eyes of children becoming young adults and parents themselves were the natural changes that occur, but as Robert Orben said, "Time flies. It's up to you to be the navigator." So, she took the pen to paper and decided to be her own navigator.

The decision to create this legacy did not come easily but was something she thought about privately for months. Her thoughts consumed her. She constantly asked herself why she was going down this path, its purpose, and what could carry forward as the world continued to change. Three simple yet powerful little words were the most dramatic and life-altering re-invention of her life. She determined these three words represent her brand, thoughts, and legacy.

As time elapsed, she decided to test the waters and see what others thought of her plan. She surveyed those closest to her on their thoughts about her vision and chosen words. She listened carefully to their feedback. And, with the grace and pose she always possessed, she thanked them for the upside and downsides of its usage. She ultimately decided to use her words.

When she first used the words, it brought surprise and questions from those she used it on. They didn't feel that she needed to do this, but true to her belief that this was what she wanted to use, nothing could stand in her way. She ultimately turned doubters into missionaries of her vision and words. She used her heartfelt and passionate three words for the remaining years of her life. In closing, those words were present in her emails, letters, and texts to all her daughters, family, and friends at the end of every day. She chose to live the life she had and mentally knew that she would never feel stuck.

My mom, the 75-year-old in this story, is our kid's grandmother. She is no longer with us, but memories of her and her one heartfelt choice are never too far from my heart. One of the best gifts we were ever given was her three words. Love, Hugs, and Blessings.

To honor and keep her memory alive, we carried it forward to every text, to/from every sister, every evening. Of course, Grandmother always spelled it out; Love, Hugs & Blessings. The sisters have shortened it to LHB. In our collaborative book, The Marshmallow Mystery, a children's book written from one of the stories shared by our dad. You will also notice it is on Jack, our teddy bear's foot. A story that keeps Grandfather's stories alive.

You are never too old to reinvent yourself! What three words are you leaving behind?

Envisioning Grandparenting to Create a Magical Childhood

Growing up, my father was the disciplinarian. Although he never struck us, he threatened us with his belt or the pida, a Polish paddle defined as a wooden handle with leather straps. Again, he never hit us, but we were not allowed to defy the rules of the house.

I grew up in a strict Polish Catholic environment, with thoughts of breaking the rules were not tolerated. However, our home was filled with unconditional love. But after becoming an adult and having kids of my own, the dynamics changed. No longer was my dad concerned about spilling milk or calling my sister a pig. He was the fun grandfather, with continual pranks and antics developing a close relationship with his grandkids. This role of grandparents is what I would like to be when the grandkids arrive.

Early on, my dad would gladly carry his grandchildren around the house, pointing out different items' names to expand their vocabulary to assist with their child development. The prank, however, was humorous. He intermittently would shake his head No, up, and down, which should have represented Yes. And then, he would shake his head side to side and say, yes. This amusing change in the truth of mannerisms brought a quizzical look to his young grandchildren until it did not. Our middle son, advanced beyond his inexperienced eyes of a six-month-old, did not question the oddity but cried at the confusion. Our young son knew something was not right, and immediately, then and there, grandfather's prank stopped.

My lesson learned was even though jokes to young children might be humorous, the intent was to bring wonder and magic to the world, not confusion. My dad's intention was not evil but meant to be whimsical. I took note of the lesson and plan on whimsy, not misunderstanding in learning with my future grandchildren.

The type of whimsy I would like to perpetuate is with our beloved marshmallow bush. Every morning beginning in spring, grandfather would make sure there were marshmallows on the garden bush for the kids to pick during the grandkids' visit. Magically pink, green, and blue marshmallows would bloom on the tree ripe for young children to pick. Yes, ants may have invaded the soft pillows of sweetness, but like any other edible garden fruit, the kids brushed off the nuisance and ate the sweet treat. The magic of grandfather's garden marshmallow bush is remembered by all grandchildren even today.

But there were other magical times invented by my father to engage in children's play. Our boys enjoyed digging with their trucks getting dirt on themselves and everywhere else. His idea was to give them a purpose. When they dug a hole deep enough, he mischievously put eggs in the dirt. Although they were regular grocery store eggs from the refrigerator, the story evolved into dinosaur eggs that were cold and needed to be warmed to hatch.

The excited grandchildren snatched the eggs gently from the hole to place them in the oven for warmth. With the oversite of their grandfather, they patiently waited for dinosaurs to hatch. Curious neighbors came to see the event, but grandfather assured the young children that they too could dig deep into their garden to find their dinosaur eggs. Our neighbor's parents quickly came to inquire about the excitement. Fortunately, they went along with the mystery of the dinosaur eggs that never did hatch.

Not all the eggs at grandfather's house were intended to hatch. During the Easter holiday season, brightly colored eggs filled with treats dangled from their oak tree's barren branches. Inside the plastic eggs contained treasured jelly belly, jellybeans. Most of the candies were deformed since they purchased them in bulk from the nearby Jelly Belly factory's store, which carried the rejects. As the children carefully tasted the delicious treats, they tried to guess the flavors. Analyzing their color did not give the flavor away since a white jellybean might have a coconut or sour milk taste. The tutti-frutti colorfully speckled bean might also taste like stinky socks. Who was brave enough to enjoy a treat or experience the unknown taste that might await inside the egg?

The activities that my parents did with their grandkids were brilliant but also had some unforeseen consequences. One time when they were babysitting the boys, they decided to buy a disk sled. Since they only raised mild-mannered girls, the thought of various uses didn't come to mind. The boys, however, conspired toward an indoor version. Caught off guard, the oldest flew down the stairs in their new toy, a disk sled, aka stair sled. Although no emergency room visits were required, the sleds were quickly accosted for only outdoor play.

But as I reflect on some of the creative antics my parents played with the grandkids, I wonder which ones I will pass down to my grandchildren. I plan to skip the yes/no confusion and the sled fiasco, but I plan to continue the dinosaur egg hunt. With our farm having 280 acres to dig around in, my only restriction would be not to dig in the cow cemetery, or they might get a surprise. Hanging plastic eggs filled with jelly belly treats would be easy to continue, but I would also like a new tradition to pass along.

With all the snow we experienced this year, getting out of the house for a good old fashion snowball fight would be fun but not very magical. However, I did come across a Winter Snow Toys kit where you could build penguins and heart shapes in the snow. Maybe hang the hearts from the tree for Valentine's Day? Or use the penguins to decorate with bird food to feed the large array of wildlife around the property. We could then sit by the fire and watch from afar the birds, squirrels or even a black bear enjoy the winter treat.

Since we live on the historic family property, I often think of telling tall tales about ancestorial ghosts. Although some young kids might be intrigued, others might be spooked, not wanting to return to the farm for a visit. Maybe sharing the tale of the Indian village that was located just beyond the creek would intrigue the old and young to be keeping an eye out for Indian fossils and maybe a distant ghost or two.

I have a little time until the little grandbabies arrive, I can dream up all kinds of magical activities to share with them and to save as a resource for grandparents. The objective is to create a sense of wonder and joy, much like the marshmallow bush did with my kids. It was a bonding time with grandfather. The one thing I know for sure, there are marshmallow bushes somewhere on our property waiting to be picked by little munchkins.

How do you plan on bonding with your grandchildren as well as your adult children?

5 Secrets of a Confident Grandparent

Shhhh, mums, the word!

Confidence is underrated. So, let' change that! What is confidence? The Oxford dictionary says it is "a feeling of self-assurance arising from one's appreciation of one's own abilities or qualities." For this story, we will refer to confidence as your specific lifetime experiences, best practices gathered, and legacy that only you bring to the table.

The role of a grandparent is ever-changing. With this change comes a new, unknown role that has been thrust upon us. My personal journey into grandparenting could be considered a minefield. This minefield began where my child married and then added a child into the mix. Or just adding a child into the mix brings about the same outcome.

So, what are the secrets to a confident grandparent? First, acknowledging that there are landmines that you will be facing. Yep, landmines. However, with the confidence that you possess, you will be able to successfully identify which of these land mines you can safely pivot around, those that might quiver as you approach, or those that can blow up in your face. Hopefully, we will never have to face those that blow up but rest assured, even with that outcome, there are ways, with confidence, that you can come out of it strong.

Take a little trip down memory lane with me. When we were parents, we were in charge. I personally didn't realize how powerful it was. We decided how we would influence and raise our kids, their religious beliefs, family values, sibling relationships, work ethic, activities, and interaction with the grandparents. Complex, yes, but...

Being a grandparent is more complex than just being the mother or father, where you write the household rules. Looking back, I see that my confident parents, now grandparents understood that there were 2 key interaction points. The first, interacting with your child's spouses', the second, collaborating with the "other" grandparents who bring their own traditions, raising styles, and priorities.

If you want to be part of your grandchildren's lives here are my 5 secrets:

1- Don't act jealous of the other grandparents!
There may be one grandparent with closer geographic proximity to your grandchild or one that is currently not working a full-time job that could be more interactive than you. If you feel like you are the "odd man out," the jealousy gene may show a little paranoia and rear its ugly head. Comments like "OMG, why did they give **MY** grandchild that ugly hat or toy or sweater?" or "how come they are always around when you finally do get some time with them?" This is typically a response of someone that might think that the other grandparent is more loved or matter more. That is further from the truth. It's not a competition — it's a family.

As Elsa sang in Disney's movie, Frozen, "Let it go." But I would edit it a little and add, "Let it go, and have a plan." Find something that you can do with your grandchild that is your time together. A holiday tradition that is yours and yours alone. Possibly a book a week zoom where you and your grandbaby read a book together or play a game or solve verbal puzzles.

2- Keep quiet!

The child you raised, put all your blood, sweat, and tears in, and given your lifelong commitment, are now on that same journey. Probably in the first 6 months, at least, of your child's new role of childrearing parent, there were perhaps alarms and sirens that went off as if they were offered a world class spa gourmet dining unlimited premium drinks and pampering experience and opted instead to stay at a hostel. Whatever the thoughts that are ready to pour out of your mouth, keep it to yourself. Our only job is to give support, not anxiety.

Sometimes opening your mouth is imperative if you believe that your grandchild is in danger. Danger typically involves food that might not be safe to eat, plugs that might not be covered, or even stairs that aren't blocked for a toddler to plunge headfirst down the flights. Dangers that aren't potential dangers are giving your unsolicited opinion on Montessori vs. public school, how they choose how holidays are celebrated, or even if they decided to buy your grandkid a car. Sorry to disappoint but these are not dangers.

I'm not saying to be quiet but rather find some nugget, something positive and supportive of their decision. Trust me, this will be respected.

3 - Your child and grandchild are different
Perhaps your child had colic or never slept through the night, had a beautiful head of hair, was a vegetable hater, or even walked at 9 months. Just because that happened to your child doesn't mean that it will be the same fate as your grandchild. So, while stories are exciting and support is valuable, constantly referring to your own parental traumas and victories doesn't help the current state.

Remember that your child and spouse have their own fears, concerns, and apprehensions and our job as grandparents is to support and reassure.

4- Break the rules...
As a child, one of the coolest parts of staying at my grandparent's place is that my bedtime was not as regimented as it was at home; I got special treats that were usually not part of my family desserts and eating cookie dough while creating cookie masterpieces were part of the daily fare.

Obviously, my grandparents were breaking clear rules set by my parents, and if my parents had an issue with it, I never knew.

I am not encouraging breaking the rules but rather promote transparency with their parents. Also, you must ask yourself, are these the activities that you and your child participated in? Are they harmful?

Honesty and explaining the why will go a long way and remember never to use the "it's our little secret" because trust me, it won't be your little secret for long.

5 – Share the stories
We are a wealth of stories, pictures, and legacy that no one will know if we don't play it forward. Before smartphones captured hundreds of images a day and geo-tagged them with dates and locations, there were printed pictures. If you haven't digitized them, make that a priority. Your kids may not know that they want them yet, but they will eventually regret that they don't know who Aunt Midge is and how she is related to them.

I am not however, recommending the conversations are about, "back in the day, I walked to school in the dead of winter, uphill 10 miles, both ways." I recommend incorporating stories that share family history and record them. Maybe play table games of what it like in the '60s, '70s, etc., or creating a book on Shutterfly on life of "me." There are numerous ways to keep the history, the family, and the memories moving forward.

A quote from a "B" spaghetti western that I remember is: "they say we **die twice**. Once when the breath leaves our body, and once when the last person **we** know says our name. Find a way to keep your name and your stories going forward.

FUN THINGS TO DO

Talk:

Tell everyone the name you want to be called and why you selected it.

Tell the story on the names used by the grandparents who came before you.

Recommend to Read:

- The Berenstain Bears Grandparents Are Great 2 book set – Stan & Jan Berenstain
- All Grandparents Love Their Grandbabies – Zoe Michal
- Grandma Loves Me! -Marianne Richmond

Questions to Ask:

When you become a grandparent what do you want to be called?

What are the special things you want to learn from me?

Describe something new you would like us to do together.

CORE VALUE: AUTHENTICITY

Embracing your unique qualities and using them to create your own path in life is the root to keeping the family strong.

Talk Date:

Books:

Stories:

Questions Asked:

Chapter 2

"Family is not an important thing. It's everything." Michael J. Fox

What's Family

The Importance of the Extended Family

My Auntie Jean just recently passed away at 101 years young. As the family's matriarch on my dad's side, she buried her husband, one son, five brothers, and two nephews over the years. Not to mention all her extended family and friends, which included my mom.

Aunts and uncles can be like second parents, while grandparents share a different type of love than the parents themselves. Cousins can also be like siblings; we have one cousin, Renee, who is like a sister since we grew up so close and have memories we share as if we were sisters. She even calls our mom "Mom." Every Sunday growing up, we had dinner at our aunts, uncles, and cousins' houses, never going out to a restaurant since so many of us were there. 7 in our family, 8 in one family on my dad's side, and 10 in a family on my mom's side. And with so many mouths to feed, a restaurant was never an option.

Thanksgiving and Christmas Eve dinners were always my favorites, even though there was an adult's table and a children's table at Thanksgiving. Not sure if I ever made it to the adults' table since there were so many older than me growing up. There was a secret veggie dish my aunt made several of every year, and we took a platter of it home with us, and sometimes there was some left when we arrived back home. At Christmas, we all assembled in the basement of my Bushi's and Auntie Jean's house, and it was informal and there was Polish food galore, cousins everywhere and fun for all. My older cousin, a firefighter, always dressed up as Santa, which was a big hit with the younger relatives.

History, too, is an essential factor to consider when raising children. When children understand and know their family history, they feel more in control of their own lives. For example, knowing how my grandparents made it from Poland to America has made me proud to be Polish, please jokes aside. Or stories from an aunt or uncle about their past helps children feel they are a part of something bigger. Learning about life in previous eras and generations and the hardships they overcame helps children learn to cope with their issues. These conversations are priceless, as the memories and wisdom carried by older family members will one day be gone.

It is giving us another reason why children need families that include a mother, father and grandparents including the entire extended family. It's a way to connect the dots and put together the puzzle pieces.

As I look back to my aunt's funeral, my heart is warmed to spend quality time with cousins. Oh, the stories and memories we had to share. With her passing, the matriarch position was passed on to the oldest female cousin, we are now the next generation and will create new traditions to share with our children.

You know that we wrote a children's book, The Marshmallow Mystery, which was about my Auntie Jean's brother Carl, our dad. She did have the opportunity to read the book before she passed, and I think she liked it since it was a story about our past that was shared with the world in a children's book format.

Let's never forget that the extended family performs several essential functions, but mainly it socializes our children, provides emotional support, and provides our children with a social identity.

Another great way to interact and connect with extended family members, particularly older generations, is to gather and share and record memories. How can you record your family's memories for the next generation?

Raising Kids in 2022: What Grandparents Must Learn in a New Era

Thinking back to when I grew up, life was simple. Not only did I play outside with no adult supervision, I remember playing in the street. We played tennis, kickball and even baseball in the street. As cars would come, we would step aside and resume the game after they passed. When the streetlights came on, we headed home. Walking a mile to school at four years old didn't seem unusual at the time. Or our summer excursion to the library to pick out books were all unsupervised. In first grade, I was responsible for walking home from school to make my dad his lunch. I would arrive at an empty house, except for our dachshund, Jadwiga. On the menu, soup, and sandwich. My mom pre-made the sandwich before she went to work; the soup, however, required a can opener and heating it up on the stove. All this taught me responsibility, independence, and confidence. However, things changed when I became a mom.

In the late '90s, we lived briefly in a small town in Nebraska. It wasn't unusual for five and six-year-old kids to have the same responsibility I had in the '60s. Kids played in the street, walked home from kindergarten, and yes, they were home by themselves. Being a protective mom, I wasn't comfortable allowing that kind of responsibility for my young children. Granted, it was a small town, but when we moved to Chicago, things that were allowed there would not be allowed today.

Letting kids play outside on sometimes questionable equipment without supervision was common, myself included. The children could walk to a neighbor's house or ride their bike without me tagging along. Car seats only lasted until pre-school since you cannot carpool with that many car seats. We let our kids walk around barefoot in the summertime. They didn't seem to mind the gravel or hot blacktop. They could set up shop with a lemonade stand to earn some cash; our kids were 6, 4, and 3 at the time. My four-year-old was a wiz with counting money by then. Let your three-year-old rollerblade in the street? Yep, the joy on our youngest's face as he would race down the road. He enjoyed playing roller hockey in the street too. However, I did put my foot down to toy guns and un-educational cartoons, which most parents allowed in that era. The only exception was at Grandmother's and Grandfather's house, where they watched Tom and Jerry.

Did they get hurt? Yes, they broke bones and had cuts so deep they needed stitches. We were regulars at the ER. Did they get lost? Yes, but that wasn't because of lack of supervision. Our middle son would purposely wait until I was distracted to wander off. I would often say nobody would snatch him since he would scream bloody murder. But, we didn't worry about our kids being taken back then. We had neighborhoods filled with kids whose parents were not hovering but home if the kids needed anything. They were also taught responsibility, independence, and confidence back then, even though I was much more protective than my parents 30 years earlier.

Fast forward to 2022, where parenting is a whole different ball game. In the last couple of years, children have been experiencing life without other children since COVID quarantine. An entire generation will be impacted by who knows what yet; brain development, social issues, and speech delays? Some parents are coping by "podding" their kids with a small group of friends. It requires children and adults in the pod to follow strict safety protocols, such as mask-wearing and social distancing, when they are in public or interacting with others outside the group. When we were raising our boys, we limited TV and computer time. Today it isn't unusual for kids to be in front of a screen six or more hours a day.

Outside of the pandemic, there are also some significant changes in how children grow up today. My kids grew up with google searches, but today's kids are growing up with Alexa and Siri. In the 1990's we didn't talk to our kids about the environment. Although we didn't litter and we recycled, it isn't the same social conscious attitude of today. Some parents and kids are going to plant-based diets. Since plant-based foods are more widely available, it is easier than when I tried to serve my kids veggie hotdogs, which they quickly spit out. Parents today are talking about gender neutrality and fluidity. Parents are starting to move away from gendered toys, clothing, pronouns, and names—not to mention dramatic gender-reveal announcements, which was never a thing in my day.

But similarly, I gave my boys toys that consisted of baby dolls, barbies, and trucks, which were purposeful for serious rounded playing, not a stand for gender neutrality. No guns were allowed in the house, plastic or otherwise. We didn't attribute any of their behavior as "boys will be boys" They could not fight or wrestle, which today would be called being "good humans." This way of raising kids seems to mirror how we raised our boys, but the reasons behind them changed: Climate Change, Gender Neutrality, Being a Good Human.

Technology and science have changed, but also terminology. We called parents that hover over their children helicopter moms. Now, the term is Spec Ops Mom, who track their kids electronically. Snowplow or Bulldoze Parent is when a parent plows through everything to ensure their child succeeds. What about the Sharenting Parent, defined as one who always has their phone out capturing an image to share. There are terms such as birthing parent instead of mom and human milk instead of breast milk. But words such as Permaculture, Freegan, Hothouse, and Climate Emergency are listed as the latest trends.

As grandparents, we can now reflect on the days gone by with what is called "free range" play. But instilling values through the next generations is still possible. We want our children to pull our values forward, but they will have their own beliefs. Look at the values of responsibility, independence, and confidence. This generation is teaching their kids responsibility to the environment. Independence by teaching gender neutrality. And confidence by demonstrating being good humans. Does it matter how they reach the same conclusion to the values you and your parents were raised? Instead of judging your children's new role as parents, learn the technology, terminology, and trends in parenting. It might not be as different as you think.

Stop Peopling: Kids Coping with Anxiety

In today's world, there are many reasons to be anxious; the war in Ukraine, the Climate Crisis, the Rise in Crime, the threat of being Cancelled, Inflation, Unemployment, and COVID. Anxiety is a feeling of fear, tension, or unease, typically about an upcoming event or something with an unclear outcome. But some children suffer from this disorder even without these impending doom and gloom events. Clinical anxiety is a nervous disorder characterized by excessive uneasiness and apprehension, typically with obsessive behavior or panic attacks. It is a chemical imbalance. Sometimes, the person suffering from the affliction needs time to stop peopling and getaway.

Our middle son suffered from anxiety starting at a very young age, although we didn't recognize it. His usual sweet, kind, laid-back demeanor turned from pleasant to tantrum when surrounded by groups of adults or kids. It was a sensory overload for him. At one and two, he couldn't express his apprehension with people. As time progressed into pre-school, he would throw a tantrum at drop-off. But as recommended by the teachers, he needed to get over the separation anxiety, so I left him on the ground having a fit. Little did I know that it wasn't me that he felt fear about leaving, but the children in the classroom. He had social anxiety.

According to the Mental Health Foundation, "Social Anxiety Disorder (SAD) is a longstanding and excessive fear of social situations. Beyond the typical sensation one might expect when speaking in public, meeting people for the first time, starting at a new job or school, or giving a performance, when the discomfort or feelings of shyness result in anxiety, fear, or avoidance and have an ongoing impact a person's daily at work, in school then it could be SAD." In children, the Foundation characterizes the symptoms as, "refusing to talk, temper tantrums, crying or being clingy with their parents are all possible symptoms in children who are anxious about talking adults."

Our son never went through the terrible twos but went through the horrific threes, a sign of anxiety. He would say school was hard as he grew, but we soon realized it wasn't the lessons. It was the crippling fear of being judged or humiliated. One of his classmates in second grade commented on a belt that he wore. He never wore it again. One school event had parents come in for the reading time. My son squirmed and shifted in his seat the entire time. He does not have dyslexia which would be another type of anxiety when reading aloud. Although he was a proficient reader since 1st grade, his concern was with the children and parents watching him. He had a feeling of being embarrassed and self-conscious.

There were many other examples of social anxiety that I missed. I had a call from the school to meet with the music teacher. Our son refused to get in front of the class to play his instrument. They didn't know if he was defiant or scared. Another time he was confused when a speech he made to his classmates had comments that they couldn't hear him. He spoke too softly. His response was, "I could hear myself just fine." But the most prevalent sign was his ADHD-like behavior, tapping the pen and shaking his leg. Since I already had a son diagnosed with ADHD, I thought he had similar issues, but I was wrong.

It wasn't until college that anxiety became a severe issue. It affected our son's schoolwork. Being away from his family, on his own, must have been scary. He was always an intelligent and responsible child, so we didn't worry about him until we had to. One night/morning, at about 3 am, he abruptly woke us up. He discovered he was on academic probation. He was not eligible to take summer school or classes in the fall semester. The school's policy was to take time off for a semester. Fortunately, he just took a psychological assessment. Since he was struggling, we thought he might be dyslexic like his brothers. But instead, it was discovered he had social anxiety.

Mustering all of his courage and determination to stay in school, he met with the head of the engineering department, his major. He met with the dean of students. He bravely discussed his issues with anxiety. Then, he sought help. We were fortunate to have The Linder Center For Hope in our town. He was able to see a psychologist, and he decided with them to begin medication for anxiety. He spent the summer interning as an engineer, taking art classes, and re-evaluating his priorities.

There is hope for children and adults suffering from social anxiety. First, we must take away the stigma of mental disorders. It is real and if the medicine helps, take it. Second, get away from people; take a walk, hike, or run. Meditate, do yoga, or do other relaxation exercises. Other calming habits can be found on The Holderness Family Website.

If you are a parent or grandparent, join the movement. May is Mental Health Awareness

Month. Learn about kids' mental health, the signs, and what to do about it. Erase the stigma. "Try to be the rainbow in someone's cloud," Maya Angelou. What is your mental health story?

No Soup for YOU

Made famous by the Soup Nazi in a Seinfeld episode and is now an exclamation used in the event where someone changes their mind about giving something to someone else. The word "soup" may be replaced with the object at hand; the reference to the show can still be unmistakably recognized if the speaker uses the correct tone of voice. The episode depicts a soup restaurant, which has stringent rules, which results in customers being denied their soup order with the line "No soup for you." This episode was inspired by a Manhattan soup restaurant's chef *Ali Yeganeh*.

We have come a long way since 1995 when this episode aired, or have we? Since Adam and Eve, denial has existed. Do you want to get your children and grandchildren to listen without nagging, yelling, or reprimanding? Instead of the "no soup for you" approach, threatening time-outs, counting to three, or denying them a beloved toy or snack time treat, use a positive parenting approach to correct your child's behavior. This approach, in time, will help with the childish misbehavior that adults dread.

Positive parenting experts worldwide can agree on this: there is always something that motivates a child's harmful or disruptive behavior. There's always a reason for the conduct. As a parent or grandparent, your challenge is figuring out what's underneath that frustrating behavior. Once you identify the root cause of the issue, you can become more proactive in order tp prevent the outbursts from happening in the first place. Children need positive attention. If they do not receive positive attention from family, they may choose to seek out negative attention. This reaction is because negative attention is still attention, and for a child, any attention is better than being ignored. Remember to communicate with your child.

Children like hugs, cuddles, and holding hands. It makes them feel secure, protected, and loved. Physical attention sends a message to your child that you show them that you are present and send them love through physical awareness. So please give them the nurturing they deserve.

May is Mental Health Awareness Month, including our psychological, emotional, and social well-being. It affects how we think, feel, and act. It also helps determine how we handle stress, make choices, and relate to others. Mental health is important at every stage of life, from childhood and adolescence through adulthood. If your child is having problems with anxiety, there's plenty you can do to help. Above all, it's essential to talk to your child about their stress or anxiety and give them solutions to deal with those issues.

As a child, our parents never discussed the topics mentioned above, and I wish they had discussed them to my sisters and me. They assumed we were five perfect children, which I'm sure we were not. I was quiet in grade school. When I was in first grade, I talked out of turn and was turned over the nun's knee, and she spanked me in front of the class. Did I ever say another thing out loud throughout my school years? No, that was not the positive response I needed. However, on a more positive note, my grandmother would give us 25 cents to sing a silly Polish song, and I would always sing it straight through and show up my cousins.

Even after visiting Poland several times in my life, I just recently found out that almost every Polish meal starts with soup.

So, my new saying is "Go Get Soup for YOU."

Grandma or Busha? Which one are You?

Or maybe you are a grandpa or Jaja? Traditionally, families in Poland were three-generation affairs, with grandparents, parents, and children sharing a household. Typically, this was a patriarchal structure, with adult sons living with their parents and adult daughters moving to the households of their husbands. The older generation held the greatest authority. This was very common in the Polish community I grew up in North Chicago, IL.

Irish names for grandparents have not been widely adopted by the non-Irish, as the German

Oma or the Italian Nonna have been, probably due to the difficulties of spelling and pronunciation. Most Irish children call their grandmothers Granny, Grandma, or Nana, sometimes spelled Nanna. Nana seems to be the most popular choice. Irish grandparents value staying independent and active. Many of them live alone rather than with family members. When elderly individuals do require care, their caregivers are usually family members. We also found this true with my husband's family which had Irish roots and had lived alone until his dad needed his sisters as caregivers for the last few years of his life.

After you and your grandchild are comfortable with your special new name, bask in all the joy of bonding with your grandchild, but without the stress of having to raise them. To make the most of this special relationship, don't worry so much about dispensing advice to their parents, and focus on taking every opportunity you can to create memories with your grandchildren. It is very tempting to buy the latest game or toy and see their face light up, and that's fine. But experiences you share are often far more meaningful and will create memories that last a lifetime. My mom, Grandmother to our girls, pulled out my old toys from her attic and they still fondly remember these experiences to this day. She taught them the game Rummikub which is still a family favorite to play.

My dad, Grandfather to our girls, put marshmallows on a bush in the backyard every morning when they visited him at the lake. The girls would rush out to pick the marshmallows that grew overnight, and it was documented with pictures over the years. However, one morning, he forgot, and the girls were disappointed. As I mentioned earlier, two of my sisters and I wrote a children's book called "The Marshmallow Mystery" published on Amazon. This is the first book in our Can You Find, Did You Know series about our dad and his relationships will all his grandchildren at the lake house. Fishing, storytelling around the fire pit, and woodworking with the grandsons to name a few.

My husbands' parents were called Grandma and Grandpa by our daughters and oh the memories that were made over the years since they were only 20 minutes away and not in the Northern suburbs of Chicago like my parents. Grandma was a great cook and made pies to perfection. She taught our oldest how to make pies and shared all her recipes with her. Mainly pumpkin pies, and apple pies and our daughter still make them every year at Thanksgiving and Christmas. She too makes them to perfection. Grandpa was a true character, his stories over the years were told over and repeatedly. We all listened to them as if it was the first time, we heard them. On the 4th of July, he would take the American flag off the house and wave it in the street as a flag send away. Yes, the girls thought it was funny, but his neighbors thought otherwise.

Memories, whether you are a Grandma, Busha, Jaja or Grandpa should be experiences your grandchildren will remember and passed down to the next generation. Cooking and storytelling, yes, flag-waving send away maybe or maybe not. How do you plan to create memories?

FUN THINGS TO DO

Talk:

TALK about your family tree and where all sides of the family came from. Go back as far as you can or spend time researching your ancestors with the grandkids. Because family matters most, and communication and history are key.

Recommend to Read:

- Me and My Family Tree by Joan Sweeney
- My Grandma Lives in Florida by Ed Shankman
- Who's in My Family by Robie H. Harris

Questions to Ask:

What does family mean to you?

What is the difference between friends and family?

What would be a fun family event?

CORE VALUE: FAMILY:

Family can offer support and security coupled with unconditional love.

Talk Date:

Books:

Stories:

Questions Asked:

Chapter 3

"We respect our elders. There Is wisdom
that comes from experience, and I am not
going to stop learning from wise counsel."
Mary Balogh

The Power of Eldering: Sharing Wisdom Across Generations

Why Grandparents Bring Wisdom

If you are older and you know it, raise your hand!

If you didn't raise your hand, I would share that once you get the "grandparent" moniker, you will be relegated to the "old" category. Yes, I know that it may be far from the truth, but as they say, perception is reality. A check of the Merriam-Webster Dictionary tells us that "The definition of old is advanced in age or having been around for a while."

There are other ways of saying old, some demonstrating gentle respect like elderly, mature, older, or even senior. Still, others may not say it to your face but could also use the words older than dirt, ancient, grizzled, or even senile.

However, what isn't always thought about that comes with age is the positive impact that a close relationship between a grandparent and grandchild can have on the happiness and well-being of the entire family. As we journey proudly into this new realm, some valid and exciting reasons being a grandparent is cool, and here is why:

#1 – Your kids can use you as a babysitter

A polite society would call that an affordable childcare option. While both parents in many families work outside of the home, the grandparents often play a vital role in raising the younger generation. According to the 2019 Census, roughly 2.7 million grandparents provide for the basic needs of a grandchild, while even more take care of their grandchildren regularly. If they are willing and able, having a grandparent with a flexible schedule act as an occasional babysitter gives many parents a great sense of comfort, knowing that they are leaving their children in capable and caring hands. Wear this hat proudly!

#2 – You can influence their lives

There are many studies out there telling us about grandparents' role in the lives of their grandkids. The most recent one I read was that 9 out of 10 adult grandchildren felt that their grandparents influenced their beliefs and values. I know that mine did!

That feeling of emotional intimacy, unwavering support, and never-ending stories helped me formulate a positive and interactive relationship. As a child, Grandma, grandpa, and even older family members gave me a perspective of how I was more than a moment in time, and there were essential connections to the past. Even the legacy I was destined to carry forward, all woven together with teaching moments that demonstrated a healthy and normal relationship. We do genuinely impact our grandchildren's lives.

#3 – You know stuff!

Don't underestimate yourself!

You are a valuable resource because you have a lifetime of stories, experiences, and perspectives that you gathered from your own life and the lives of people that came before you. You may intimately have interacted with your grandparents and relatives, but they are only "great-grandma or grandpa's" names on a family tree from the next generation's perspective. We have the tremendous responsibility to share the depth of the past and take them from only a name to a family legacy with tales that our grandkids can carry beyond our years. That link to our grandkid's cultural heritage and family history is priceless. Children understand more of who they are and where they come from through their connection with us. Wear that experience proud!

#4- Security Blanket

Grandbabies will eventually turn into grand teenagers! Especially valuable during the challenging teenage years, having an extra layer of support can make a huge difference in this child's life. Again, numerous studies show that solid grandparent-to-grandchild relationships show there are fewer emotional and, yes, even behavioral issues if the grandchild has a safe sounding board to open up and share the problems they are facing. The grandchild may think these problems are overwhelming, but with your experience and listening skills, you might just become their go-to person to talk to.

I remember firsthand that there were times that my mom or dad "just didn't understand me" or would tell me something that I didn't want to hear, and I would run to grandma to get her viewpoint.

Thinking that she would side with me, I looked back and realized that I received the same response my parents gave, but I somehow "heard" and understood the reasons from a different lens. Grandparents provide a sense of security.

#5 – Grandparents don't sweat the small stuff

As a parent, sometimes we unintentionally became "helicopter moms or dads." As that "old" person in the room, we, on the other hand, have seen much, experienced more, and survived to talk about it.

We can reduce household stress if we have an emotionally close relationship with our grandkids. Teaching our grandchildren to brush off the little things that might occur sets them up to deal with the tough stuff as they grow up. Knowing they have another sounding board to deal with life's issues and a trusted companion and help them see the wonders of life is my single most joy of being a grandparent.

So, in closing, I encourage you to "be cool" and enjoy your role as a grandparent. It's one of the best jobs in the world.

Growing to be an Elder, Not an Older

What is the difference between an elder and an older person? According to Webster, an elderly is a person who is old or who is aging. And if you look up the definition of old, it is described as having lived for a long time, no longer young. But the difference is an earned and respected position in the family by having a growth mindset.

In various cultures, the elderly have an elevated status. In Japan, they are generally treated with the utmost respect. Many traditional events are held in their honor, showing the gratitude of the younger generations. In the American Indian community, the elderly are considered the "wisdom-keepers" and are held in the highest regard in the community. They are the protectors, mentors, teachers, and transmitters of cultural knowledge. Greeks in America and Greece don't have the shame around aging and death. The Greeks honor old age and celebrate the elders as the center of the family. Calling someone an old man is not a bad word in Greece.

Why does Western culture have such a stigma about aging and death? Psychologist Erik Erickson argued that the Western fear of aging "keeps us from living full lives." But this attitude about aging lacks the concept of "the whole of life. " While other cultures accept death as a fact of life, Western civilization is entrapped by fear. As Elbert Hubbard said, Do not take life too seriously. You will never get out of it alive."

"And the beauty of a woman, with passing years only grows!" Audrey Hepburn.

Carmen Dell'Orefice, the oldest working model, solidifies that claim. At 91, the silver-haired sensation even posed nude for New York Magazine. To her, age is just a number. Kathie Lee Gifford professes not to have retired but to be re-fired. She is supporting a healthy lifestyle to keep herself young. So age is not about getting older; it is an attitude of a growth mindset.

On the surface, aging is growing older. But with a growth mindset, you can grow elderly. An elder comes with life experiences but is wise enough to understand that they don't know everything. Take, for example, technology, I feel pretty savvy for someone my age, but to a millennial who was raised on technology, I am a neophyte. When I had internet problems and asked my computer programmer, son, for help, he said, "watching baby boomers do technology is painful." Maybe a valid point, but I am learning every day and not afraid to fail; I have a growth mindset.

An old person might be unable to hear very well, or they talk about the good old days, not keeping up with the times. An elder person listens. They pay attention to what the rising generation has to say. I enjoy the vast knowledge of my adult sons. I am proud that accumulated so much knowledge in this Digital Information world. They taught me just to google it when I want to know what something means or how to do something. We depended on encyclopedias in the day. Google or Alexa is much more convenient. Listening is a skill that a growth-minded elder has by learning from youngsters.

Elders have discernment; they can make keen observations about things. Armed with their life experiences, they can step back and see the bigger picture. Take, for example, watching grandchildren grow. Elders can wisely observe a grandchild's struggles and share their own struggles at that age. My kid's grandpa shared the story of how he couldn't qualify for a prestigious school based on his entrance exam. He had a disadvantage, dyslexia. But he studied hard and retook the test. The admissions officer said it wasn't enough to be accepted, but he never saw such improvement in such a short period of time; he was accepted. The lesson of not giving up even though school is hard has stuck with our boys, especially with their own challenges with dyslexia.

An elder has a growth mentality that can bring the gift of wisdom, family stories, rituals, traditions, and the family's values to life. An older person who looks at life in only the past deprives the family of their family's legacy for the future. Watching my mom grow into elderhood, I have a role model to follow. Are you living as an elder or as an older? Who is your elder mentor?

Grandparenting Isn't Just Frosting on a Cake: Why Grandkids Need their Grandparents

When I reflect on my parents as grandmother and grandfather, not mom and dad, they were the fun ones with the grandkids. They were not how I remember my mom and dad growing up. They were the disciplinarians trying to keep their five daughters in line. Where are you going? Whom will you be with? Be home no later than midnight since "nothing good ever happens after midnight." But with the grandkids, they didn't have that responsibility. They could teach them to fish, tell stories about magical fairies, and bury "dinosaur" eggs for the kids to find. They had endless treats like ice cream, cookies, and cupcakes with extra frosting. But grandparenting, I have learned, is much more than frosting on cupcakes.

Grandparents link the past to the present, all while helping grandkids find their way to the future. The grandkids' parents were kids once too, who might need to be reminded about their youth. Maybe little Tyler is running around crazy, swinging from the trees and jumping in mud puddles, just like his dad. Or Sage is spinning in her twirly dress, dancing to the music in her head, just like her mom. But it is also reminding them of their heritage. Aunt Kathryn, the businesswoman in the 1920s, had that entrepreneurial spirit like her grand-niece. It is the responsibility of grandparents to join the links to the past.

The grandparents remember the patriotic duty of the country. America united during WWII, rationing items for the country's sake and serving to preserve freedom. Their service and sacrifice earned them the title of the Greatest Generation. There are still survivors out there from the Holocaust who can attest to the atrocities. And we need to honor the veterans at the WWII War Memorial. A meaningful field trip to take grandkids on (or great-grandkids).

We must recognize that the Grandparents earned their stripes. This isn't their first rodeo. As my mom used to say, "I might not know now or know tomorrow, but I will eventually know the truth." They have probably heard or seen it all. A three-year-old temper tantrum, yep. A nine-year-old punching a hole in the wall, yep. A teenager not coming home after prom, yep. They can be the sounding board for handling a difficult situation— a different point of view.

Grandparents provide a sanity break for parents. Drop them off at grandmother and grandfather for a week of summer camp. In our case, it was called Camp Cadillac, where the kids could swim, fish, and kayak. A perfect option for those parents balancing work and family, especially in summer. I know many grandparents who provided homeschooling during times of crisis—a huge relief for parents struggling with doing it all. But even during regular times, grandparents can be that extra hand for before and after-school childcare or simply a date night for the parents. What is more fun than going to grandmother's and grandfather's house for the night, weekend, or a week of camp?

Giving children a perspective on overcoming a loss would benefit grandparents. A child could have a simple loss of a teddy bear or a friend that moved away. However, it could be a significant loss of an aunt, uncle, or parent. Grandparents are role models on how to overcome grief and move on with a good life. The pain may not leave, but the child will learn that life goes on and it is okay. Grandparents, at this point, would most likely have buried their grandparents and parents, to name a few. I personally have been to more funerals than I can count. Each one brings grief and tears, but it is also a time to celebrate the person that passed away.

We know that preaching doesn't help parents or children, but leading by watching, listening, and asking questions is a grandparents' gift. When we pay attention to our grandchildren, we can notice things that a parent or teacher might miss. Observing that little Mason doesn't know how to rhyme could be the first sign of dyslexia. Listening to little Peyton cry about his lost stuffed Froggie teaches empathy and compassion. Asking about not just Tyler's day at school but his grass-stained jeans, ketchup on his shirt, and paint on his face allow grandchildren to recount the joys of the day. Being a noticer can bring an outside but caring perspective.

A grandparent cannot solve various difficult family situations, but they can help build the grandkids' foundation for the future. Like a cupcake needing a solid base before the frosting is put on, the family needs a strong family unit. Grandparents provide those ingredients for the parents to mix together. One without the other won't make a good cupcake. Although grandparents are more than just frosting, it is the frosting that is fun and oh-so-sweet. And that is the added benefit of grandparenting, fantastical frosting to create a close relationship with grandkids.

Grandma's Washing Machine

What can you learn from Grandma's wringer washing machine?

If there's one household appliance most of us could not do without, it's the washing machine. We all need to use them. Most of us use it at least once a week. We may have to drive to a laundromat, go down to the basement, or down the hall to complete the washing function. We gather our dirty items and carry them judiciously to our laundry area, load the machine and entertain ourselves for 45 minutes before we move our items to the dryer. But the dryer will be a story for another day.

So, what does a washing machine actually do? A quick Google search explains it as putting in dirty, unfavorable clothes, swishing them around gently, adding a little soap, putting them through the wringer, hanging them up to dry, and good to go.

What?? That's not how my washing machine works! You are right; that is the washing machine of the 1940s.

You are probably wondering what a washing machine has to do with intentional grandparenting but stay with me on this journey.

Taking a little trip down memory lane, did you know that the old wringer washers did not spin? You wash first, wring, rinse and wring again. So, what this machine does is the heavy work of swishing: no settings, no timers, no fancy buttons, and spaces for bleach or softeners.

The washing machine I am referring to is my grandma's. It somehow made its way down a rickety set of stairs to a dark basement where a single light bulb gave a shallow hue as you loaded the machine. Now, this washing machine was not a Bose, Whirlpool, or even a GE front or top loader. This washing machine was a vintage wringer wash machine with industrial strength build in metal enamel. Its girth was dirty white and broad. The opening for the placement of the items was square and wide with an agitator so large that it filled the entire bucket. But it is the top device that was the most unique and mysterious. To the modern eye, it looked like a pasta maker plopped on the top of this humungous machine. Looking at the front it appeared that it was smiling mysteriously and knowingly at you.

As all grandmothers previously, they found lessons in the most obscure place and weaving them into day-to-day activities that teach you without lecturing or guilting you into submission. A piece of advise that will last you a lifetime.

Her washing machine was her vehicle. As a child, it was my honor to bring down the rags to the mysterious basement and start the process.

The task of gathering the dirty items, mostly rags, was my weekly activity, and interaction with the washing machine was a life lesson. The simple act of filling the machine with those rags, making sure the water level was at exactly the right level was the first step. As in life, a washing machine overflowing with rags (aka work) will throw off our balance and if the water level is above the manufacturer's guide (God), the machine would rock and shake and possibly even dangerously shimmy across the room.

However, it's the wringer that is magical. Since the wringer is a manual process, it is through the action of grabbing the item that needs to be placed in the wringer is cathartic as we naturally think of each of the issues that had us spinning earlier in the agitator. The wringer could only handle a few items at a time. If you selected poorly (bad decisions) the machine would tell you immediately. Too few items and the rollers couldn't pull out the excess water. Too many items stuffed in at once and the roller would creek and even stop, forcing you to re-group and re-think your actions. Personally, I never was able to truly master the art of putting just the right number of items in the wringer.

So, what does a wringer washing machine have to do with being a grandmother? As this grandchild got older, I learned from her that shortcuts make long delays and that making mistakes is ok. You haven't really lived if you have never experienced something not working out as you had planned. Being human does not come with an instruction manual, a how-to-be-perfect guide.

Outside of museums, there may no longer be wringer washing machines, but there is a treasure trove of day-to-day activities that we can give to our grandkids that can teach life balance, making mistakes, and changing as lessons are learned...all without using an app.

Grandmother's Apron

Growing up in a Polish American house provided the opportunity to an array of Polish cuisine. From homemade Polish sausage and pierogi to my favorite dessert, potiza, pronounced (paw-tee'-tzah). I remember it as a tasty bread with a sweet, nutty filling. As I reminisce about my favorite foods and memories, I picture my mom and grandma cooking diligently for the family feast. My grandma with her house dress, and my mom in her slacks, both adorned with an apron. This nostalgic look at the past had me thinking about the lost item used in cooking, aprons. What were they used for, and why are they no longer in everyday use?

Did You Know? The primary purpose of aprons is to protect the clothing of the cook. It uses less material than our clothing, making it easier to clean. If you splash something during preparation, the apron prevents you from making a mess of your attire. Our parents and grandparents didn't have the abundance of clothing most of us have today, so they couldn't necessarily make a quick change. They also tended to have larger families leading to lots of dirty clothes to wash; any help decreasing the laundry load is a significant benefit. And don't forget their dryers were outdoor clotheslines.

Another benefit of wearing an apron is to prevent your food from coming into contact with dust, dirt, hair, germs, and whatever else might have been floating around you throughout your day. I would think there would be an apron shortage if people realized the advantages of the apron.

There is also the safety issue that encourages apron attire. If you have an outfit that contains polyester, which was very popular in the 1970s, your clothing could catch fire. But there are other concerns, like wearing anything big and loose. Also, baggy clothes could catch fire too or get caught in mixer beaters or other equipment.

Back in the day, aprons were used as potholders to remove hot pans from the oven. They also were absorbent, so they could gently dry a child's tears or quickly clean dirty ears. Gathering eggs from a chicken coop could be easily carried in an apron. And when the company came, it became a hiding place for shy children.

After a long day over a hot stove, an apron was used to wipe the sweat. And if it got cold, the apron doubled as a shawl, draping it over the shoulders. When you needed to bring in the wood, the pieces were carried in by that very apron.

An apron carried all kinds of vegetables from the garden into the house for washing. If peas were shelled, it carried the hulls in to be disposed of. In the fall, apples picked or fallen from the tree could be hauled into the house for apple pie or homemade applesauce.

Need to clean the house quickly for unexpected guests? The apron saves the day. It is amazing how much furniture an apron can clean. It also doubles as a wearable dish towel.

Remember never to throw away an apron because aprons hold memories! That stain from coloring Easter eggs with your grandchildren or the rip from carrying a heavy load of firewood to make s'mores. And if you have an apron with a pocket, all the most precious memories are hidden there too!

From cooking and carrying to cleaning, this handy dandy article of clothing belongs in the new age of sustainable necessities for the home. It is like a superhero cape, ready to tackle today's messy world or to cook with your grandchildren. Forget about your grandmother's apron and house dress; create your look and make memories today.

How to Alter Ageism: The Last Tolerated Discrimination

Ageism is defined as prejudice or discrimination based on a person's age. This bias can vary from blatantly aggressive behavior, either physically or emotionally, to benevolent patronizing. In a world of social media's fake but glamorous model-like looks, grey-haired wrinkled people seem to be pushed into the shadows. Their wisdom through the ages is often ignored or not given the respect it deserves.

Baby Boomers are often regarded as a low-tech generation since they were not raised in a digital age. However, it was this generation that created the PC and the internet. Steve Jobs was a pioneer of the personal computer era transforming telecommunications. Sir Tim Berners-Lee, who created the World Wide Web, is also a boomer and considered one of the greatest inventors of all time. And we cannot forget about Bill Gates, who launched Microsoft. This generation's wisdom shouldn't be regarded as lacking tech savvy.

On the other hand, there are still people from the Baby Boomer generation that do not have internet access. Not having access is the dividing line of digital acumen. It isn't that they cannot learn technology; they just don't have access. This fact became clear during the COVID-19 pandemic. Vaccines were only scheduled via the internet. Not having it became a health issue. But given access and training, the Baby Boomers could do everything from online browsing to TikTok videos.

By 2030, all of the Baby Boomers will be over the age of sixty-five. This age, for many people, is considered a retirement age. But long gone are the days of sitting in a rocking chair with an Afghan crocheting a sweater. With the largest amount of personal wealth, this group can travel the world or do anything else they want to do.

But instead of buying bigger houses, this age group is downsizing. They might want to age at home, "the ability to live safely, independently, and comfortably in one's own home and community," they are frequently relegated to senior living centers and nursing homes. During COVID-19, these centers were locked down for their own safety but left the elderly lonely and abandoned. Segregation of a population would be considered discrimination against other groups.

However, the solution is easier than it seems. Even if they don't currently realize it, the younger generation has much to learn from the wisdom of the Baby Boomers. The trick is in the approach. As a Boomer, Are You Eldering or Oldering? If you want your grandchildren to learn some of your life lessons, are you listening to them? It is a two-way street in sharing each other's knowledge.
Millennials and Gen Zs grew up with technology. Helping those in the previous generations become more technologically familiar and fluent

will improve the self-worth of both parties. What skills can you share with your grandchildren? Do you sew, play the piano, or even cook? All the basics that could have been missed during the hectic screen time generation can now be shared.

One of the most valuable activities for the rising generation is storytelling. When grandparents tell stories about their grandparents, the multi-generational value lessons are passed along. Yes, telling them about how you grew up without the internet and walked to school uphill both ways can always get a laugh. But telling tales of how your great-grandfather was in an explosion at the Sugar Factory that sent him flying through a window where he landed on a train that took him downtown Chicago is a true tall tale that won't be forgotten.

"Mom, Can We Visit Grandmother and Grandfather?"

With all of the bustle in our daily life, escaping to their grandparents' magical house is a much-welcomed break for grandkids and parents alike. After trekking the kids to soccer practice, gymnastics, lacrosse, and archery, to name a few, we parents and kids need a break. And the answer is not Disney or the beach but to grandmother and grandfather's house.

Grandmother's and Grandfather's house is where the pendulum of handcrafted clocks tick and tock rhythmically, but time seems to slow down.

Grandmother's and Grandfather's house is where the smells of fresh chruściki, or angel wings, fill the kitchen, enticing the children. Their big smiles and white powder sugar faces wait patiently for more.

Grandmother's and Grandfather's house is where the little ones wake up early to pick squishy marshmallows from their special bush.

Grandmother's and Grandfather's house is where an attic filled with old-fashioned toys is discovered. The eternity of playing with tinker toys or Candyland then ensues.

Grandmother's and Grandfather's house is where making sandcastles and digging for treasures is part of the daily routine.

Grandmother's and Grandfather's house is where fish are caught to children's delight. Proudly their pictures are taken and hung on the bulletin board of memories.

Grandmother's and Grandfather's house is where an enormous dollhouse is available for boys and girls to play endless imaginative make-believe scenarios.

Grandmother's and Grandfather's house is where painting the white picket fence is an opportunity to learn the importance of hard work and patience.

Grandmother's and Grandfather's house is where we discover the relics of our parent's childhood and the beginning of our lives.

Grandmother's and Grandfather's house is where it is possible to discover dinosaur eggs filled with jelly bellies and other mystical magic that nobody questions.

Grandmother's and Grandfather's house is where hugs are given, showing the deepest affection, and everything is allowed.

Grandmother's and Grandfather's house is where watching Tom and Jerry and other cartoons are not prohibited but encourages giggles from little amused faces.

Grandmother's and Grandfather's house is where water mysteriously streams through an old-fashioned red pump only when Grandfather is around.

Grandmother's and Grandfather's house is where soda and ice cream are abundant, and bellies are filled with Jell-O jigglers.

Although Grandmother's and Grandfather's house is only a fond memory, it will live with their grandchildren for a lifetime. Someday, I want my grandkids to experience the wonder and magic of their Grandparent's house and the wisdom that comes from time spent there.

FUN THINGS TO DO

Talk:

TALK to your adult children and explain to them the importance of grandkids spending time with grandparents. It is beneficial for the kids to learn family values and for the grandparents to stay healthy, happy, and sharp.

Recommend to Read:

- A Morning with Grandpa by Sylvia Liu

- When I Am Old with You by Angela Johnson

- Grandma's Purse by Vanessa Brantley-Newton

Questions to Ask:

What do you think it would say if you found a message in a bottle at the beach?

What things do you like to eat but don't get at home?

What is something that helps you fall asleep at night?

CORE VALUE: RESPECT

Listen to your elders. They may not always be right, but they have more expertise on being wrong.

Talk Date:

Books:

Stories:

Questions Asked:

Chapter 4

"Inside each of us is a natural-born storyteller, waiting to be released."
Robin Moore, author

The Importance of Storytelling

The Rocker: Where Stories Came Alive

The soothing sound of a rocking chair's gentle, rhythmic creaking and squeaking. A warm, rich, and slightly sweet scent of tobacco and smoke-filled air from a worn, chewed pipe. The comfort of sitting on my dad's lap while listening to his stories about his travels through Europe during World War II. These are the magical memories of my childhood.

As far back as I can remember, I have been fascinated with Switzerland. Not just from the stunning mountain scenery, picturesque cities, and mouthwatering chocolate but the stories my dad fondly talked about after his time in WWII. A country that remained neutral but was also located at the center of the conflict was intriguing. The country became a refuge for scientists such as Albert Einstein. After serving in the army and fighting in the Battle of the Bulge, my dad took a leave in Switzerland. He received a book to commemorate the visit, which was the basis of his storytelling.

By crafting his story, he shared a piece of his life when he was young. He served his country, which probably had unique narratives, but the joy of traveling to a peaceful nation was the topic of the tales. It was inspiring to hear about the adventures of a youthful soldier exploring new places. "The World is Yours," he would say encouragingly to me, his tiny daughter, who was learning to read. The time spent rocking, listening, and dreaming was how he shared a bit of himself.

The stories also built on our father-daughter relationship. Switzerland, known for its timepieces, provided endless tales corresponding to my dad's clockmaking passion. We would spend hours in the basement working on clocks: antique, granddaughter, grandfather, and cuckoo clocks. The Swiss cuckoo clock cultivated my imagination. The gingerbread-type house, adorned with intricate carvings featuring woodland creatures and scenes from nature, provided countless discussions about traveling to see these chalets tucked into the Alps.

These narratives also taught me creativity, problem-solving, and cultural awareness lessons. And the benefits of storytelling, if he knew it or not, improve children's language skills and memory. But 50-plus years later, I remember bonding with my dad. Fortunately, I also have the book that started all the stories as a memory.

"You are the storyteller in your own life. And you can create your legend or not." Isabel Allende

Overall, storytelling is essential for parents, grandparents, and educators to help young children develop their language, cognitive, emotional, and social skills. However, it was my dad's way of inspiring me. At six years old, I wanted to go to Switzerland. Yes, I did go there, but he mainly passed on the adventurous spirit to travel and live in various places since "the World was Ours."

Do you want to be an inspiring storyteller? A good story typically has the following pieces: conflict, tension, surprise, controversy, mystery, suspense, and extraordinary characters. Crafting one can take time, thoughtfulness, and creativity. But the best stories are those shared with your grandchildren about your life growing up and the lessons you've learned. Not just the successes but the failures too. These will last a lifetime. Leaving a legacy through storytelling is your superpower. Go make memories.

The Fire Princess and her Secret Realm

Did you ever meet a fire princess?

Some of you might think that meeting a fire princess would be easier to do as a child, but I didn't have the opportunity to meet one until I was well into my 20s. She appeared unexpectedly one evening, and I quickly learned a fire princess could always be called upon.

Now, I don't remember ever seeing her while growing up. She may have been hidden in plain sight or maybe didn't appear until after the kids were born but appear she did. And she enchantingly emerged for each of the seven grandkids and the five sisters.

What made her so special? Well, her magical powers occurred as she danced in the fire pit flames at grandfather's house. She could entice and engage our imagination and creativity with a simple whisp of a flame. Her skill? Using grandfather as the conduit, she painted a picture of a parallel universe, unique beasts, and challenges that needed to be faced and won. She confidently overcame every encounter she faced, and she would engage others to help win her battle. We willingly joined in the fight.

Our fire princess was not the only imaginary character we encountered. The events at grandfather's house are legendary. There was always something that sparked each kid's imagination, activities that challenged the status quo and often allowed everyone to look at the world differently.

The legend of the fire princess is just one of the tales magically created by our dad, the wise and powerful spirit of legend and legacy. He was a master storyteller. Professionally trained as a machinist, you might not think that was a career that prepared you for the skill of storytelling, but he taught us that there is a storyteller in each of us, regardless of your background. Just take a breath and look at your surroundings with awe and innovation, and the stories will emerge.

The fire princess was just one of his many stories, all steeped in mythology and symbolism that mesmerized us all.

Since our fire princess's initial appearance, she became a significant figure in the evening narratives. After dinner, we would all rush out to the fire pit. As the sun set, our dad would fuel the fire with the traditional wood, but as the flames and sparks began to fly, the fire princess appeared.

Each sister and grandkid would probably tell a different story about what she looked like and what message she was sharing, but everyone saw her and felt her power.

The impact of our unique fire princess has been far-reaching and long-lasting. Her appearance has helped shape the narrative of many of our books and has provided a platform for other grandfather tales. We hope that she inspires you as you become your family storyteller.

Abracadabra: Bringing Magic into Grandparenting

Busy parents juggle job, budgets, and their children's crazy schedules. Waking up before sunrise to take a child to hockey practice and then toting them to the soccer field seems to be my world. Organized activities from swimming lessons to gymnastics are packed into the parenting schedule. Fielding work calls from the game sidelines are just part of the work-life balancing act. Life can get complicated when you multiply that by more than one child. But if a grandparent is available, they can not only ease the burden of the daily routine; they can inject some magic into a child's life.

Our father, my boy's grandfather, is a model for creating enchantment and wonder out of the mundane. Take an ordinary egg, for example. This everyday household staple turned into a dinosaur-saving adventure. Because the egg is cold (it came right from the refrigerator), it needed heat to nurture the creature inside. An oven could act as an incubator for the tiny dinosaur. Not too hot, but a low temperature for just enough warmth.

Where did the dinosaur egg come from? While the boys were digging in the front yard with their Tonka trucks, Grandfather cleverly put the egg into a hole in the ground. When Grandfather gleefully exclaimed, "You found a dinosaur egg!" the boys happily believed the tale. Of course, this caused chatter with the neighbor kids, who also wanted to find their own dinosaur egg. After hours of digging in their backyard, they returned frustrated and eggless. But with encouragement from Grandfather to persist and keep digging, they returned to their task. Fortunately, good-natured neighbors appreciated the tale and encouraged the imaginary story.

Make-believe is an integral part of the serious business of play. It encourages not only imagination and creativity but for kids to think for themselves. The magical play will develop their social and emotional skills as well as their language ability. The ability to think abstractly about an object other than the ordinary meaning will grow with this type of play. Depending on the activity, it can build small and large motor skills from digging a hole or picking marshmallows off a bush.

Caring for the dinosaur egg demonstrated empathy for other creatures. It showed the wonder of a potential birth. It was respecting nature and being concerned about something besides themselves and a sense of responsibility to all life forms, big and small. All these values Grandfather exhibited instead of merely talking about them.

How do you become that Abracadabra grandparent? Take your cues from your grandchild. What sparks their interest? When my boys were little, they were obsessed with dinosaurs. At two years old, they could name them all. Grandfather understood their passion which directed his creativity toward this magical adventure. But if dinosaurs are not of any interest, choose something more enticing to that particular grandchild such as unicorns or puppies.

Once you have identified their interest, what values do you want to teach? If you are trying to teach patience, gardening might be an activity that engages your grandchild. To add magic, plant some marshmallow seeds into the mix. If hard work is a trait you want to instill, have them help you paint a fence. But add the fairy-tale about the magic paintbrush for some mystery. To teach self-confidence, paly challenging activities like a scavenger hunt, "Can You Find?" They can find everyday items like a hat or something more challenging like a concept (i.e., something with a pattern or something bigger than your hand).

The Abracadabra moments in your grandchild's life are treasured forever. The values learned from you will be irreplaceable. But the bond that develops between you and your grandchild is priceless.

Not Just a Toy, But a Movement

When you were a kid, would your parents allow you to play with a 5'9," measurements of 39/18/32, and a size 3 shoe?

My parents would, and I even played with more than 1 at a time!

She allowed me to spin stories and create different scenes involving all sorts of imaginary characters and adventures...or misadventures. Storytelling has held a special place in people's minds since the dawn of time. When we were kids, we made up our own stories to make sense of our world or take us away to foreign lands.

Alright, she may have been my Barbie doll, but she was so much fun. Throw in my Ken doll, and the adventures expanded even further. Whether a princess or adventure story, the stories felt so real that I could quickly feel an adrenaline rush in my veins as if I was living it out.

I am not here to debate Barbie's incorrect body dimensions to what a typical human woman looks like. Truth be told, as a kid, I never actually thought about her size at all. I knew she was not shaped like a baby doll and could go places and experience things that no baby doll could ever do. After all, those baby dolls always needed to be put down for a nap.

So, playing with Barbie dolls was a great way to stimulate my imagination and creativity. But that was never enough. I had the luxury of 2 younger siblings who, hidden in the cubby hole under the stairs, surrounded by a Barbies pink convertible, house, and plethora of clothes, would continue the tradition of creating intricate stories involving moving parts and different scenarios. Watching them create stories like these and escape into fun-filled dreamlands was an absolute blast.

Why am I talking about kids and their vivid imaginations? Because the encouragement and support start with you. Kids need stories as much today as ever, not just tales told by adults – kids should be taught to tell stories themselves!

We have all played with toys and have stories to share, but we are failing our grandkids if we believe we are the only storytellers in the family. Storytelling is integral to any culture, even in this digital age! Stories are often how grandparents connect with our grandkids. Sharing stories about our childhood, yes, but what about getting down on the floor, or in the cubby hole, under the stairs and creating stories together.

You can help them to practice storytelling techniques, like setting a scene, building suspense, and delivering a punchline. From classic fairytales to stories from our families - all stories matter and help kids understand their world better. Who knows - maybe your kid will be the next storyteller-extraordinaire for the next generation!

By honing their storytelling skills, kids can deepen their understanding of the world at an early age and build connections with parents, grandparents, and friends. Grandparents especially love to hear stories from their grandchildren - it's always a fun bonding moment for them!

Yes, Barbie revolutionized how kids played with toys all around the world. After all, stories like Barbie are timeless.

The Mouse Ate My Mail: Creating A Tall Tale

Going to the mailbox is typically a non-event for most everyone. But living on a farm, we are always in for nature's surprises. Have you ever found a visitor? Would love to hear your story.

Our morning routine is to leave our house, drive up our long farm road, and get our newspaper and the mail on the way to the gym. I cross the street carefully that no cars or pickup trucks are coming down the winding road. I fling the door open quickly when I approach the mailbox, usually startling a mouse or two snuggling inside.

This particular morning was a challenge since the mice didn't seem to want to leave. The shreds of the mail piled up in a cozy next for the two dwellers of the mailbox. As I shoed them away, I noticed the tiniest tiny newborn mouse in the corner. No wonder the mice were reluctant to leave; they protected their newborn. But can I leave them be and use the excuse that the mouse at my mail instead of the dog story?

Did You Know the phrase "the dog ate my homework" comes from an English expression that schoolchildren make as a common, poorly fabricated excuse to explain their failure to submit an assignment on time? Even beyond the educational context, the phrase is referenced as sarcastic. Much like the excuse "my dog at my homework," a mouse explanation might be considered false. However, the destruction of my mail is now a daily struggle.

I asked USPS about my dilemma. They recommended aluminum foil since mice supposedly hate the foil. Unfortunately, our mice find it a decorative addition to their next – the shreds of aluminum sparkle amongst the dull pieces of mail.

Peppermint is another recommendation. Instead of killing the mice, it offers a successful natural remedy that works to repel them. It has to do with the nature of mice; they rely on their sense of smell instead of their vision. Mice have an incredibly weak vision but a robust and keen sense of smell. That makes sense why mice typically go for a large chunk of stinky cheese, right?

It brings to my mind the book, "If You Give a Mouse a Cookie." A circular story about never being able to make the mouse happy. The tales continued from the author who subsequently published, "If You Give a Mouse a Brownie," and "It's Pumpkin Day, Mouse," In reality, it should be if you give a mouse a piece of stinky cheese or other smelly foods. Maybe that would have satisfied the mouse instead of a cookie, brownie, and pumpkin. But to spark the imagination of children, it is the tall tales that stimulate their interest.

So, the mundane task of getting the mail can become an adventure for a child. I decided to focus on the peppermint route for a "Did You Know" lesson by explaining the factual information about mice's sense of smell. Then, a children's story about mice to be read out loud. I recommend, "Mouse in the House." Since the story's theme is to get rid of the mouse instead of making it happy.

You can create your own story about "The Mouse in the Mailbox," By supplying children with paper and crayons, and their imagination, a tale is brought to life.

If you don't actually have a mouse in your mailbox (lucky you), you can always buy a cute plush one. It can become a game of "Can You Find." You could put it in the mailbox or the house. An exercise similar to the Elf on the Shelf but played year-round.

This concocted fairytale can be created with many day-to-day, seemingly dull events. "Give a Mouse a Bath," could explain how mice are good swimmers. Did you know they can swim for days on end? "Mouse Manners Matter" can be a name of a story about teaching manners. And "Adding Bling to a Mouse Home" can conjure up a tale about aluminum foil decorations. The possibilities are as endless as you and your grandchild's imagination. Make up a tall tale today! You might even solve the "Mouse Ate My Mail" story. But at the very least, you will develop a bond with your grandchild that will last a lifetime.

FUN THINGS TO DO

Talk:

Share stories with vivid description of your ideas, beliefs, personal experiences, and life-lessons, these experiences will help light the way, encourage the little one's curiosity and give them insight into your life.

Recommend to Read:

- Grandfather's Journey by Allen Say
- Uncle Jed's Barbershop by Margaree King Mitchell
- The Sunsets of Miss Olivia Wiggins by Lester L. Laminack

Questions to Ask:

If you could meet someone from the past, who would it be?

If you wrote a book, what would it be about?

If someone were to write a story about you, what do you hope they would write as the last sentence?

CORE VALUE: CREATIVITY

Creativity is inventing, experimenting, growing, taking risks, breaking rules, making mistakes, and having fun.

Talk Date:

Books:

Stories:

Questions Asked:

Chapter 5

" You just don't pick up family values,
unless your parents teach you and let
you know exactly what they expect."
Brian Lara

Family Values

Pulling Forward Not Pushing Forward: How to Perpetuate your Family Values

As a youngster, I was raised in a family business, a mom-and-pop convenience store. My mom started work at 5:30 am every morning, even on Christmas. She brought in the newspapers, opened the cash registers for the day, and straightened the shelves to ensure everything was in order. She would continue the day by waiting on the customers, restocking the shelves, ordering new inventory, and scheduling the other family members' work schedules since only family worked in the business. Endless amounts of cash would go in and out of the store, trips to the bank for deposits, and stacks of bills to count. As early as six years old, I would join her at the store to help before school. Throughout my childhood, I learned our family's core values by working alongside my mother.

I learned Integrity by watching her handle money with accuracy and honesty. Counting the money repeatedly while placing each bill in the same direction, she demonstrated her character. Never did she steal even a penny from the register, even though money was tight. The bank, at times, was even wrong in their count, trusting my mom's truthfulness to their error. She exhibited the behavior she wanted to instill in her children instead of pushing her values on us.

Work Ethic, a typical Polish trait, was also displayed at our family business. My mom never complained about the abundance of work required to manage the business while juggling raising five daughters. I cannot say she was the best cook, but we had food on the table and clean clothes for school. She laid our clothes out the night before, so there was no need for further discussion in the morning. She had a system for everything, which kept her efficient and the family on task—checklists for cleaning the house on Saturdays for those that didn't go into work that morning. Designated chores for who set the table, swept the floor or did the dishes after dinner. We didn't get an allowance for at-home duties, but we did earn an hourly rate when we worked at the store, even if starting wages were ten cents. We didn't complain, and we were happy to work hard for the sake of the business. Her work ethic pulled forward the perseverance core value for the next generations.

Where family started and family business stopped never had a clear distinction. The family was first, but it intertwined in our daily lives of running a business. My mom didn't have the opportunity to pursue her dreams but rather help where help was required. As the third generation in the business, she established herself in a key role in the operations. But the dream she had for her daughters was to see the world. She would often say, "the world is yours." She didn't push us into the family business but allowed us to pull forward the value of family.

To perpetuate the family core values, first, you must demonstrate them in your daily life. Proclaiming your values without modeling the values will not establish them in your children's or grandchildren's life. Having a vision, mission, and core values statement for your family gives the family direction. Unfortunately, if the next generation doesn't have key input, it will be imposed on them instead of established within them. Trust the younger generation to give insight as to what is important to them. Collectively the family can generate core values that give meaning to the family.

Our adult children chose Family, Integrity, Perseverance, and Knowledge to represent our core values. These reflect what my parents passed along to us. Although my parents always stressed the importance of education, our children felt Knowledge was more inclusive. Education seemed to stand for a formal structure of learning while Knowledge included experiences of life. Having our children pull forward these values gives me hope to pass along the lessons I learned from my parents and grandparents to future generations, my grandchildren.

What are you actively doing to help your grandchildren pull your family values forward?

Price of Success: A Grandparents Perspective on Achievements

Parents inherently want their children to succeed. They stress the importance of "excellence" for their child. As a baby, they may start teaching their child baby sign language to bolster their cognitive ability. They can be eager to sign up their three-year-old up for ballet or, in this case, for wrestling. Yes, as a parent, I am guilty of arranging for art classes, gymnastics, swimming, and more, all before the age of four. As parents, we fear not having that jump-start will forever put them behind in academia, the arts, or sports. However, as a prospective grandparent, I have a different viewpoint.

Questioning our children's actual ability first came from a talk by the Olympic Development Program (ODP) coach for soccer. He asked the parents, "Who has ever competed in the Olympics?" When nobody raised their hands, he asked, "Who has ever made the national team?" Again, no parents raised their hand. He then said, "With this gene pool, it is unlikely any of your children will make the cut for the state ODP team." Although it sounded harsh, his point was not to expect perfection...excellence. Instead, please encourage your child to work hard, do their best, and not to quit at the first sign of difficulty. Everyone has different gifts, which most likely will not be revealed at three years old.

Parents often want their children to follow the parent's dream instead of the child's. Our son competed in archery through college. One of the coaches was a Gold Medal winner who encouraged his students to use their head instead of their brawn. Although his coaching was outstanding, his own son was overshadowed by his father's success. He was always the son of the Olympic medalist. When he lost a competition, he also lost his self-esteem. It didn't take long for him also to drop archery as a sport. Letting your child pursue an activity that they are passionate about instead of the ones you succeeded in or dreamed of achieving increases the likelihood of their accomplishment and happiness in other activities.

Stop competing with the Jone's child. It is a common phenomenon for parents to compare their children to their neighbors. Little Johnny Jones is walking at eight months, but your child only is starting to crawl. Or Sarah is talking in complete sentences at a year old, and your child doesn't even say mama or dada at 18 months. Today, parents rush their children into the pediatrician wondering what is wrong with their child, or they are on the other side, bragging to their friends how precocious Susie is at two years old. Looking back at our children, we had both ends of the spectrum. According to the book, our oldest seemed to be advanced in every aspect, What to Expect the First Year. Our middle son did walk at eight months and spoke in complete sentences at a year. He would say words like "Watermelon," taught by his proud grandparents. However, our youngest son never crawled in the classical style, but he got up and ran after his brothers one day. He also didn't talk until he was two years old, but when he did, his brothers asked if he had an off button to shut him up. As a grandparent, the perspective of watching a grandchild grow and develop at their own rate can bring parents into the reality of raising a healthy, happy child, not a perfect specimen.

What is the impact of pushing your child too much? According to the book, Children of Paradise, the children might suffer the wrong kind of motivation; external expectation rather than internal drive. It is a result of what the parents expect instead of their own desire to achieve. In the extreme case, The Dead Poets Society demonstrates the impact of a parent forcing his own directives on his son, ending in a tragic death. If that doesn't make you rethink your parenting style, I am not sure what will. But what can you do as a grandparent to help your child be better parents?

As a grandparent, you have more influence than you think. Of course, you don't want to interfere with the parent-child relationship, but you can encourage the child's process to success. Compliment them on working hard to try out for the school play. Point out their eagerness to learn new information. Admire their ability to ask the question, why? Even if they have asked it a million times. Note their ability to be kind, polite, and tolerant toward others. When you model good parenting behavior to your grandchild, you will see how the child positively reacts. Thus, the parents will see how to positively parent without criticizing the parent themselves.

Demonstrating good parenting techniques when interacting with your grandchild does show good role modeling. The parent might find it helpful, but they also might reject it. That is okay. They are the parent, but it can help you develop a genuine bond with your grandchild as the grandparent. The one warning I will say is not to jump on the golden child bandwagon. It is easy being a proud grandparent to say how exceptional the child is at this or that. Beware of the negative consequences of that behavior. Even comments "like father, like son" to refer to a successful parent might put undue pressure on a young child. Encourage their unique gifts and talents. Listen to their hopes and dreams, which might differ from their parent's expectations. Don't interfere; encourage.

Collections of the Past and Present

Most parents and grandparents have noticed that their kids and grandkids loved collecting things at one point or another. It could be rocks they find outside, seashells they seek out whenever they're at the beach or a specific kind of toy. Growing up, my mom and dad encouraged us to collect coins that turned into a rather large coin collection. It's fascinating why children collect things, but the main reason is that it's fun. Kids get to learn more about things they enjoy, and it's interesting for them.

Over the years, I have collected stamps with my grandparents, spoons from the places I traveled, black and white prints of towns and cities I visited, wine corks, matchbooks, and books. Until now, I didn't realize that I was having so much fun collecting all these items, and I'm sure there are more that I can't remember.

It's not uncommon for kids to be interested in a wide variety of things and collect about anything, like key chains, Pokemon cards, and Beanie Babies. Our daughters started collecting Webkinz when this plush first hit the market in 2005. Webkinz was one of the first children's toys to bridge the plush and digital worlds. The stuffed animals were sold with codes that allowed its owner to bring its pet to life and care for it in the cartoon-style Webkinz World online. When the newest Webkinz pet came out, we all jumped in the car and rushed to the nearest Hallmark store to snatch it up if it was available. If not, the hunt continued.

The hobby of collecting includes seeking, locating, acquiring, organizing, cataloging, displaying, storing, and maintaining items of interest to an individual collector.

However, this isn't the only reason why people collect things. Others do so out of nostalgia for their youth. As any parent or grandparent knows, it is common for children to go through phases obsessed with certain things. These phases can last anywhere from a couple of weeks to several years, but most of us eventually grow out of them. Yet some people never do, or they return to their childhood passions later in life. Their collection acts as a sort of safety net from the adult world for these people. It is a way for them to temporarily let go of the burdens of their present lives and put themselves back in their younger self's shoes.

To younger generations, things like record albums or DVDs hold little meaning. For others, like myself, these are the things that I grew up with. As the modern world moves further ahead, collecting these objects becomes more and more alluring. They offer a retreat back to simpler times, especially when such items are no longer produced. Of course, these objects will be all but forgotten in the future. But people will always be nostalgic for the past, and there will never be a shortage of items that evoke these feelings.

Today, toys and dolls tied in with movies are usually a big hit. These items aren't huge investments, and Disney collectibles always have a strong market. Once you've purchased a few dolls, stash them away carefully in their original boxes, and keep checking their value over the next few years. They could be the next big Disney collectible. The golden rule of collecting is to buy what you love, and if you're lucky, it'll become valuable. My spoons, matchbooks, and wine corks are long gone, but it was fun when I was young to collect these unusual items I loved at the time. What's in your collection?

War, What is it Good For?

What is new about war? Nothing...but you knew that!

Conflicts, battles, and wars are as old as time. They are fought for various reasons ranging from independence to the expansion of national borders. If we counted the American Wars, not to include the wars of others that the **US** soldiers were part of, we are currently at 12. Starting with our own fight for independence. In all these scenarios, they are all horrific, and regardless of who wins, the "losers" are the citizens whom the war takes its harshest toll.

Back in the day, the news was only shared at 5pm, 6pm, and 10pm or in the morning or evening delivery of the newspaper. Kids could be quickly sent to another room or handed the comics, making it easier to keep the gruesome news from the young.

Now, as we are currently facing, in real-time, the war in Ukraine. It's on every channel, every newspaper, and even discussion and videos in school. 24/7 war.

Depending on the age of our grandkids/kids, let's help them face the reality of today. How? Not by showing the pictures of the death of devastation but rather by playing games. No, I am not saying shove the war under the rug, but let's first teach them the fundamentals of war and strategy. The goal of the Hasbro Risk game Risk is simple: players aim to conquer their enemies' territories by building an army, moving their troops in, and engaging in battle.

As a kid, my sisters and I would play the game of Risk for hours on end. We felt defeat, were elated with victory and were driven to develop a strategy to "take the other man team out," only to learn that the roll of the dice and your early strategy allowed a player to defeat the enemy or be defeated.

In life, there is always an element of action and consequence. If children act on the Risk board without thinking it through or considering the possible effects, they could fall behind in the game and eventually lose. It does not take kids long to start realizing the correlation between action and consequence when learning in a fun and engaging way.

So, why am I recommending playing the game of Risk? It's a conduit to start the discussion on how the "luck" of a country, the strategy to stay in control, alignment, partners, and in the real world, it is sometimes a roll of the dice. And finally, the bigger bully does not necessarily always win.

Healthy competition is essential for the development of kids and adult relationships. It helps people set boundaries and get to know each other deeper. When in competition with someone else, you can see a bit more about who they are, how they behave under pressure, and their personal ethics.

Now, how deep the kids' conversation goes depends on their age. It is critically important to talk to the kids about actions and consequences and what is happening in Ukraine depicts the political situation...a real-time Risk.

Use Risk to teach kids about actions and consequences. That being said...

...war, what is it good for? Absolutely nothing.

Out-Loud Words: Don't Let Your Values Collect Dust in a Box

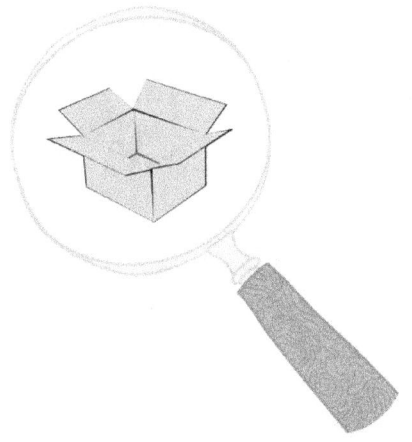

When our boys were little, we read all kinds of books together. Ten in the Bed was so well loved that the pages separated from the bindings. Polar Express wasn't just a Christmas Story but a year-round journey to the North Pole. And Good Night Moon we read as a bedtime ritual. They grew into silently reading the Harry Potter series as they entered elementary school, but our out-loud story time didn't diminish until much later. They developed a love for books and boosted their learning and educational progress.

Reading out loud sharpens young minds, boosts their listening skills, fosters their imagination, enhances communication, and much more. When teachers, parents, and grandparents read out loud to their children, they are advancing literacy development. But what if you are trying to enhance the development of their values? Can you use those same principles to install your family's vision, mission, and core values in a meaningful way for a preschooler? Or will the statement achieve scholarly excellence but end up on a shelf out of sight?

My aunt and uncle developed a Vision, Mission, and Core Values Statement for their family. It started with, "Our mission is not only to survive but to achieve. We must do so with morality, though maturity and in happiness." It continued with three more paragraphs defining what it means to succeed as a family. An impressive statement, unfortunately, life happens, and the message ended up in a box. Their eight children found it after their parents passed away. Maybe it was the big message, not the day-to-day out-loud words, that caused the statement to be lost with time.

Having exact out-loud words drives the point home to what is significant. For example, "I can do it" or "Never give up" promotes hard work and being able to endure when things get tough. In our family, we have the core value of perseverance. Since that is a big word for a small child to understand, simply stating out loud, "You can do it," reflects that value. Integrity is another, but rephrasing it as "Do what's right" can be taught to even the little ones. If you want to encourage learning, education, or knowledge, "Ask Questions" can be a statement easily understood. Remember to be patient when asked repeatedly "why." You are instilling a core value of curiosity and knowledge.

How do you create your own family's out-loud words? If you have a family vision, mission, and core values statement, you can start there. Take the adult version of the value and simplify it so something meaningful to a child.

Achievement = Think Big
Confidence = I know I can, I know I can
Courage = Be Brave
Faith = God Loves You
Golden Rule = Be Nice
Gratitude = Say thank you
Happiness = Smile
Integrity = Do what's right
Knowledge = Ask Question
Perseverance = You can do it
Trustworthiness = Speak the truth

If you don't have core values already determined, think about short, kid-friendly topics about beliefs you would like to pass down to your children and grandchildren. There should be no more than five, or it will be too overwhelming. Ask yourself, what do I think a good person looks like? What does success look like for an adult? What personal traits would you like to see once they are grown? What are other principles vital to you and your family?

Besides repeating these phrases often, use a multifaceted approach for the best retention. It is valuable to tell stories about the quoted words. As an example, for perseverance, "Remember when grandpa did so poorly on an exam that he wasn't allowed into school? He studied hard to try again and was able to do much better the next time." Stories paint a colorful picture of the lesson you are teaching. The tales can be embellished to make a point but not so far-fetched other values are compromised. You can also ask how the child demonstrated that value today. Or ask which one of the out-loud words they saw today in themselves, another student, or the teacher.

Visuals are also a means to instill the quotes. Although they might not be able to read yet, they will become accustomed to how the word looks. To accomplish this visual, have the saying on the wall in a frame or decorative writing (we don't recommend cursive). Painting stepping stones or rocks can be an attractive display. A rock can be taken along if they feel they need the reassurance of a particular value that day. Buying motivational wristbands can be used as a daily reminder to wear one or all the words and phrases. Or create with your child their visual representation of the value in a picture, a song, or other unique ways.

However, the best way to pass along your core values and what is important to the family is by your actions. If you aren't trustworthy, they will use your example over your out-loud words. If you demonstrate the opposite of what you preach, the message will be lost on tiny ears. Be mindful of living up to your values daily, weekly, and always. But most of all, don't let your values collect dust only to be recognized after you die. Live them today!

What values do you want to pass to the rising generations?

Child Labor, Grandmas says go for it!

Let's do a quick survey. How many are in favor of child labor? Against?

Child labor...these words conjure up images of children working from dawn to dusk in spinning mills, shucking clams, or spraying arsenic on cotton fields in the 19th century or early 20th century. All of us would say that we have moved to a better place. Those were horrific times, and luckily our grandchildren today have never experienced any type of dangerous work, nor should they. However, there is nothing wrong with teaching them the value of hard work and letting them experience it.

When my sisters and I were young, the leaves began to fall, and the air started to get brisk. We knew it was time to go to the farm. What did that mean for us?

It was corn harvesting at our cousin's farm.

Our job was to pluck the dried animal corn from the stalks, shuck it, and throw it in piles. Miles and miles of piles. We finished picking the fields as dusk approached, and our cousin would hitch a trailer behind his tractor. We excitedly knew our next job was to throw the corn onto the trailer as it drove by. Drive, throw, dump, repeat.

A long exhausting day, but we knew that at the end of our productive work, we would celebrate our labors with a whole pig roast. While the adults prepared our feast, the kids would head to the pig stye and play with the pigs. Note: Pigs bite, so never take up a dare to ride the pigs. Lesson learned.

These experiences will never be forgotten.

Today, the opportunities to work on a farm from dawn to dusk are slim, but museums, festivals, and county/state fairs still give children a chance to experience some of the old crafts.

This blogger still loves a simpler life, and when fall and spring roll around, I can demonstrate how to spin yarn, shear sheep, and even give kids the opportunity to pick the seeds out of cotton. Of course, before Eli Whitney's cotton gin. That was grueling work. Sadly, because of the concern for germ transfer, few of today's kids experience milking a real cow or goat. So, let's get off the farm and look around the home.

Priceless childhood experiences include hard physical work but can still be an elusive concept for them or maybe even their parents. As grandparents, we can help. If you have a garden, have them weed it for you. Down south, weeds pop up daily and grow faster than Kudzu. If you don't have a garden, I'm sure you know someone who does who would love some help. Granted, kids may end up pulling up some of the garden plants, but overall, having a child spend a couple of hours pulling up weeds in a garden can be a good life lesson. Pulling weeds without the distractions of earbuds or cell phones can encourage self-reflection or flights of fancy, i.e., daydreaming.

Look around, a friend may have backyard chickens, and your grandchild can learn to pick up eggs and feed the hens.

This type of labor is probably new to them. Still, your enthusiasm will help with disconnecting from today's pressures and reconnecting them to the more mindful world where they learn to interact with and appreciate the world around them. This simple action is powerful and one of the best things we can do for them as grandparents. Let's help them be more excited about what is happening around them when getting their heads and hands off their devices.

Your grandkids may never work on or even see a farm but teaching them the value of hard manual labor will develop good work habits and improve self-esteem. Oh, and if they are worried about germ transfer, no worries, Purcell and a good hand washing is readily available, so get in there and let them learn. Clean 'em up later.

What did you remember having to do as a child? Did you help on a farm? Milk a cow at the county fair? Did you weed your grandmother's flower garden? Would these experiences benefit your grandchildren as they grow into adults?

A Walk on the Beach...with Jesus

"Footprints," also known as "Footprints in the Sand," is an inspirational poem about having faith in God. My husband shared a popular story with me last weekend as we took a walk on the beach. The tracks represent stages of our life. Jesus promises to walk next to us, and the story describes a person who sees two pairs of footprints in the sand, one of which belonged to Jesus and another to him or herself. At some points, the two pairs of footprints dwindle to one, especially at the lowest and most hopeless moments of the person's life. When questioning Jesus, believing that Jesus must have abandoned his love during those times, Jesus explains, "During your times of trial and suffering, when you see only one set of footprints, it was then that I carried you."

Throughout my life, I have experienced many stages and crossroads. My childhood, those teenage years, college years, marriage, divorce, second marriage, and children. Each one of these stages was a blessing, and I genuinely believe that Jesus has been walking with me every step of the way. In the future, I will experience new stages and crossroads, daughters getting married, retirement, and grandchildren, to name a few. Each of these stages is a blog in itself and, in some cases, a book.

Different life experiences help you learn and grow, and your outlook on the world changes. As your age increases, so does your level of maturity. Life is a journey of self-discovery. Throughout your life, you'll find learning opportunities for becoming a better friend, partner, and family member. The growth and changes that we experience in our lives go beyond our physical being. We can develop social, self-conscious, and self-reflective capabilities. By understanding the stages in our lives and what each stage entails, you can build self-awareness and live your life with purpose and intention.

By living with intention, we set out each day to engage in meaningful activities that serve a good purpose and will have a positive influence on our lives. Volunteerism has many benefits. Making a difference with practical actions toward others can benefit your mental health. Giving back and helping others can help us feel better about ourselves. Also, remember to choose significant activities and try to live your life by your top priorities, values, and your beliefs.

A poem by Mary Anne Radmacher called Live with Intention inspired me. "Live with intention, walk to the edge, listen hard, practice wellness. Play with abandon. Laugh. Choose with no regret. Continue to learn. Appreciate your friends. Do what you love. Live as if this is all there is." Mary Anne also wrote a book that is available on Amazon.

Live with Intention: Rediscovering What We Deeply Know.

When we live with intention, we will shine, and we are all meant to shine in our unique way. We have our special talents and gifts and can contribute extraordinary things to the world. Two of my sisters and I are authors of a children's book series, and It's time for us to shine as authors. As we found out, we each have the unique talents that we have contributed to writing our first book in that series; The Marshmallow Mystery. Teamwork and working together to solve a mystery is the theme of our book. If we share good ideas, as we did in our book, we will shine as children of God and in our future life stages.

Good luck to you on your journey walking on the beach! Thank you.

FUN THINGS TO DO

Talk:

TALK to all your family members about the values that matter to you and articulate and clearly define what is expected at home and how they should interact with their community.

Recommend to Read:

- As You Grow by Kirk Cameron

- We Are Family by Patricia Hegarty

- Love Makes a Family by Sophie Beer

Questions to Ask:

How would you like to be remembered? What changes would you like to see in the world?What do you enjoy doing to help others?

CORE VALUE: VALUES

Values include honesty, integrity, generosity, courage, and confidence.

Talk Date:

Books:

Stories:

Questions Asked:

Chapter 6

"What we have done for ourselves
alone dies with us;
what we have done for others
and the world remains
and is immortal."
                    – Albert Pike

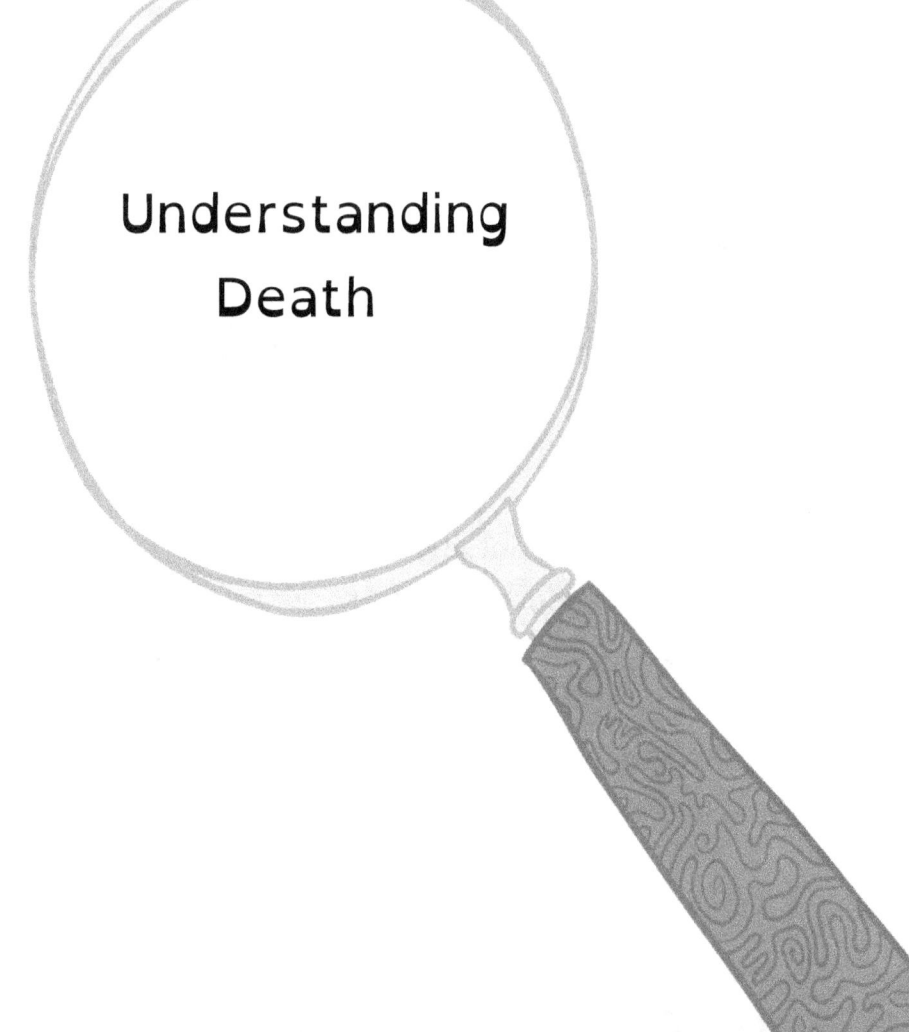

Understanding
Death

Inspiration Comes from Everywhere, even when a Matriarch Passes Away

My day started like any other; the gym, the obligatory dog walk, the never-ending conference calls, and cups of coffee...virtually Groundhog Day. Then, a quick peek at a text changed my next 72 hours and life forever. Someone died.

Now, we all intuitively know that people die. Some of them are close to us, and sometimes it's people we knew from our past; sometimes, it is farther away from our lives but vaguely familiar because of their notoriety and everything in between. Then, of course, there is the cause, some from accidents, self-infliction, disease, and yes, even old age. Each death, regardless of the proximity to our lives, brings a moment of pause. It was the passing by old age that this blog addresses. My aunt has passed away. She was less than five months from her 102nd birthday! Yes, 102.

This death, however, hit me at a level deeper than I even expected. Now, don't get me wrong, death by natural causes, with no pain, would ease anyone's angst about their final days, but this was unusual. She was the matriarch. Now, the matriarch of the family, though not me, is a cousin from MY generation. We now moved, in an instant, to the next place in the circle of life.

Think of life from 100+ years ago. From a historical perspective, this means that in the year of her birth, the roaring 20's, the jazz-age flappers' era was the rage, the first day of alcohol prohibition came into effect that lasted 13 years! As the year continues, Joan of Arc was canonized as a saint. The US Post Office said that children could not be sent by parcel. The first commercial radio station began daily broadcasting. The 19th amendment was passed where women were legally allowed to vote after 100 years of protests.

Of course, during those 100 years, she was there when TV was introduced. She saw the move to "smart devices" for our news and entertainment and everything in between. She saw changes in prices of movie tickets from .27c, milk was .33c, and a new house was $6,972.

But Auntie Jean was more than what was happening in the global environment. She was the only girl in a family of 5 brothers and was a survivor. The brothers went off to war, she stayed home and supported the family from behind. She was fiercely loyal to her family, and as her loved one's lives moved from independence to the inevitable, she became their caregiver. A rheumatoid-riddled father, a strict mother, her brothers, her sister-in-law, her children, nieces, and nephews, were her focus and passion.

She still had time for a career with the Great Lakes Naval Station, the officer's club, for over

50 years. So popular that they named a salad after her, The Belski Salad. The unofficial head of the family in a traditional family, she appeared to live her life by just putting one foot in front of another, but that was far from the truth. At her wake, I asked family members their memories of her. What I heard was awe-inspiring. The shared stories and the knowledge and insight she brought to this world influenced and changed everyone who interacted with her.

But the inspiration for me is that she did not plan to be the matriarch of the family. Instead, the role was thrust upon her by life choices, circumstances, and age. What influenced me is that she, observed everything, rolled with the punches that life threw at her, and she showed how aging is an art and not a burden, unless you make it one.

Remember, inspiration comes from everywhere. Everyone has a story. She had a lifetime of stories that will have you think and grow if you were willing to spend the time to listen. Yes, it's true. It doesn't matter if you are 10 or 102.

I leave you with one last thought. While you were waking up today, someone else was taking their last breath. Be thankful for this day, don't waste it. Inspire someone. You can make change happen today!

A Time for Heaven Story

There is never a good time to die...for anyone. As I write this my dad, who left us 14 years ago, my grandma, who left us two months before the birth of my daughter. These are just 2 of hundreds that have probably passed away that were connected to me in some way. As each of us takes a moment to think about those that we believe made it to heaven, as well as those that went to h*ll, the question of definitions comes top of mind.

There have been bullies in my life that, at that moment, I would have sworn they should never go to heaven. There are people who died too young, like my college friend who was home for spring break his sophomore year that a hit and run driver killed as he rode his bike to work. Heaven...definitely.

It doesn't matter if you are six years, 16 years, 60 years, or anything in-between and beyond. Death can change someone's life on earth forever.

But where did they go? That is a question that theologians have been pondering for centuries and still have not come any closer to the answer. So, what can a young kid and eventual adult do? How do we cope? What do we believe?

As a child, I was taught about heaven and h*ll in a religious setting. The essence was that heaven was where all the good people went after they died and h*ll where the bad people went. But what exactly is good or bad? How do you explain it, let alone explain it to your grandkids? Suppose you and or your grandkids have a religious affiliation. In that case, your religion might give you the comfort and resources to define heaven or the reasons why h*ll might be the alternative.

If there is no religious affiliation, the question doesn't change, but the definitions and conclusion can become more muddied, and therefore, the discussion with your grandkids more convoluted.

So, what do you do?

My plan to share with my grandkids starts with a discussion with my son and his wife on what they believe and what they would like me to reinforce with my grandson. Suppose they are looking for insight or suggestions on how to address this issue. In that case, I will share that another thing we can emphasize is that nearly everyone, whether they have faith in a particular religion or not, believes in the basic tenet that we should treat others how we want to be treated.

If you want your child to be treated well, despite whatever your child chooses to believe, then we want to teach them to be kind and respectful and fair to children who don't think as they do.

Kids love to play word games, particularly as you're driving around in the car or trying the pass the time waiting in line, so I would play a game called "Fact, Fiction, or Belief?" This game helps our grandkids learn the difference between 'fact,' 'fiction,' and 'belief' in terms of things around them, without making it about religion.

So, you might say, "Our car is blue—is that fact, fiction, or belief?" And you define "fact" as being something authentic, "fiction" is untrue (or made up), and a "belief" is something you think is true but can't be proven either way. So, your blue car is a fact, pink grass is fiction, and "all dogs are good dogs" is a belief.

As kids get better at discerning the difference, you can begin to tie the same concepts into different religious beliefs.
Children's books about religious stories or holidays are also a great way to introduce your kids to religions through storytelling rather than indoctrination.

I would love to hear how you deal with heaven and h*ll and your explanations to your grandkids. I would move heaven and earth to be able to explain it better.

Let's Make a Pact: No One Will Die

You are probably wondering what the heck have I been drinking to come up with a headline like this. Well, celebrating (?) the passing of my grandma, the loss of my husband, and everyone in between has caused me to ponder.

The contemplation? How to stop death!

We all have experienced crying, and I will guess that either by proximity or through the trending news, has felt death. Crying and death go hand in hand. My heart still breaks 33 years after my grandma's passing, just months before her first great-granddaughter was born. And it still breaks my heart every day, a short 18 months since I lost my husband. Crying and death continue.

However, the personal examination that is taking place is not about death. There is nothing new here. In life, there is death. But I am going to challenge the status quo. It is my mission to stop death! My secondary objective is to turn the tears into laughter.

By now, you are now probably seriously thinking that I need some serious intervention.

Let's take a breath. I know, I know that this is a tough ask and will probably get a lot of pushbacks, but I want to look at death with a different lens. I know the tears won't go away, but I challenge you, and me to bring death to a brutal stop.

So, the skills we will need to accomplish this is...nothing. We don't need any advanced degrees, don't need to be proficient in a second language, or even be technologically proficient.

We do need to tap into our collective past and dust off the primitive tools that were given to us before there were writing devices.

The minstrels of yesteryear had the magic bullet. Storytellers like Aesop and Homer, to name a few, could be seen in the marketplace telling stories informally. These two famous bards thrilled their audiences with oral tales ranging from the fall of the Trojans to fables such as The Tortoise and the Hare. When peeling back, these compelling stories are values, life lessons, and memories passed on through the ages.

For humans, telling stories is one of the most basic forms of connection to eternal life. We can use songs, poetry, videos, and yes, even a blog to tell stories. This is our opportunity to start having them passed down from generation to generation.

I would like to take credit for this epiphany, but the Egyptians believed that you die twice. Once when you take your final breath, and then again, the last time someone says your name. They believe your spirit lives on as long as people keep remembering you.

I learned about this philosophy not from prolific reading but rather from watching a B-spaghetti western 20 years ago. I don't remember anything from the movie, not even who starred in it, but I remember vividly that one saying, and it stuck with me...when our last breath leaves our body, and when our name is spoken for the last time, is when death really occurs.

As I take my first step towards not allowing anyone to die is a story about my husbands, Grandpa George Lavin. He was an immigrant whose most prized possession was 2 crystal glasses proudly displayed and gingerly pulled out yearly. Grandpa George died decades earlier, but the tradition of toasting his life lives on. My husband, Cliff Lavin, and his nephew, David Lavin Eggen, continue to honor and remember. This tradition continues as the next generation learns and toasts...Grandpa George, you are still with us. Mission accomplished.

So, I challenge you and me to use those tears to motivate us to tell those stories, tell about the laughter shared, lessons learned, and legacies passed on.

My wish for you and those you love is that they only die once. We are the storytellers.

Death is a normal but difficult fact of life. Death touches everyone, whether it's the loss of a pet, classmate or family member, or death on a local or national scale. Partner with their parents, consider the age of the child and approach the subject accordingly.

I'll Be There for You

The theme song of the sitcom "Friends", written by The Rembrandts, is appropriate for all stages of life.

"So, no one told you life was gonna be this way (clap, clap, clap, clap, clap)

Your job's a joke, you're broke

Your love life's DOA

It's like you're always stuck in second gear

When it hasn't been your day, your week, your month

Or even your year, but I'll be there for you."

Yes, your mother warned you there would be days like these, but your family and friends will be there to pick you up off of your knees. No truer words for the recent passing of my sister-in-law Nanci. She left behind a 22-year-old daughter who also lost her dad several years ago. Family and friends are coming together to console her and take care of the final estate details. My husband is the executor of his sister's estate and along with his remaining three sisters, they will figure out all the details and passwords which are quite a challenge to access her phone and computer.

I would recommend everyone read "Plan Organize R. I. P.: The Definitive Guide to Putting Your Final Affairs in Order" so that your affairs will be easier for your executor and close family members. Every page provides detailed, practical instructions for completing the big and small details with the least amount of disruption.

Maya Angelou once wrote. 'I've learned that people will forget what you said, people will forget what you did, but people will never forget how you made them feel.' My sister-in-law, Nanci, was one of those people who always made people feel loved and welcomed. She was always willing to step up and help people in need. She made everyone feel not just good, but also important and valued.

A shout out to the aunts, uncles, cousins, and friends who make our kids their own. The aunts and uncles step up, even when they are not expected to. Those who support, advise, and love unconditionally. Those who spoil, offer comfort, and become a safe space. You are so appreciated.

Moving on to the next steps of the healing process "I'll be there for you." Those are powerful words, and if you use them, be prepared to stand by them. When tragedy strikes, it's easy to be there in the initial period of need. Hugs, words of comfort, and advice for the near future, (clap, clap, clap, clap, clap). But, when you look at the actual long-term support of someone needing to be there for that person, them floating in the abbess of the unknown, be one hundred percent positive that, if you are that person, making that commitment, that you will, unconditionally, fulfill that promise of "I'll be there for you".

"I'll be there for you". So, what does that mean? It means exactly what you intend it to be. When you realize the needs of the recipient of your generosity, and that is what it is, generosity, define it and share it with the recipient. You then sit down with that person in need, and you tell them, I am here for you, and this is what I want to help you with. By doing this, you will be built a solid foundation for the relationship between you and that special person that you will be connected with by the commitment you have made of "I'll be there for you".

As you think about the concept of, "I'll be there for you", remember that there need not be a tragedy, long-term illness, or death to be able to be there for someone in your life. People in need are all around us. Just look around. Brothers and sisters, parents, and friends, (clap, clap, clap, clap, clap), you can make life-changing improvements to someone in need. Just look around, they are in need and need someone to be there for them.

Who will you be there for?

Connect with Loved Ones Beyond the Grave

No, this is not about a séance to reach Houdini. This is about you...and me. Have you thought about what you want to be known for when you leave this earth?

My mom did, I started, and maybe by the end of this blog, you will be ready for it too.

Ben Franklin said, "If you do not want to be forgotten as soon as you are dead, either write something worth reading or do something worth writing."

However, creating a simple document that will be remembered long after you're gone is another equally important component to genuinely sharing your best life. What is the easiest way to do this? Writing letters. It is a powerful way to leave a lasting legacy and share your wisdom with those you love.

Think of your kids, your grandkids. We want to show you the value of creating meaningful letters that will touch the hearts of your loved ones for years and generations to come. It is your story, your legacy, your last hug.

Why would someone what to read your last hug?

After all, you have effectively lived a full life and told your family how you feel about them, all aptly handled by you, so why go any further?

I will throw the gauntlet down and tell you that saying, "I love you," or perhaps thinking you told them your thoughts, is not enough. Period.

You probably heard the old saying no one ever laid on their deathbed and wishes they had spent more time at the office. Rather, you will wonder, "what will I be remembered for?" What people will say about you years from now and, importantly, what your children and family will pass on about you.

Your life. Your legacy. Your story. Do you want to rely on others to tell it, or do you want to help them tell it?

Why write the letter?

I call this the letter that never posts because it is designed to be written today and shared after your passing. These heartwarming messages will offer your family and friends healing, some insight, and much-needed peace that may never have previously been shared before.

Imagine receiving a heartfelt letter from someone you love and admire after they passed away. They've thought of every detail: their purpose, passions, and how they want others to remember them. By writing these letters, we live on after our bodies die—on paper and in spirit!

Who should receive the letter?

I'd start with the grandkids first, then your kids. Basically, anyone you want to influence or share a memory.

Creating a legacy for the loved ones you have left behind I think is one of the essential things in life. Helping your loved ones continue living through memories and stories is a fantastic way to remember someone who has passed away. They are not sad letters. They should provide comfort and guidance for those left behind. Write with sincerity and love. Discuss what's meaningful to you and your relationship with that person. Let the words evoke emotion and feelings as if you were talking directly to them. Sharing pieces of yourself can also give them a better understanding of who you were and how much you cared about them.

How long should it be?

As long as you would like, 500 words or less is typically recommended. The most important thing to remember when writing these letters is that it's not a comprehensive biography but a thoughtful and meaningful expression of your feelings and memories. These letters capture the highlights of your life and any memories you think should be shared with future generations. It's important that the letters focus on positive experiences and what they mean to you; it's also important that the notes are written with a warm and sincere tone that reflects your personality.

Finally, it is essential that the letters remain true to your personal beliefs and values; this ensures that the legacy left behind will be an accurate reflection of who you were and what mattered most in your life.

What can you include in the letter?

Pretty much anything, as long as it's positive. Here are a few thoughts.

- What made you proud of them.
- A special memory or moment that you had together
- Your hopes for their future
- How important they were in your life
- What they taught you
- Things you admired about them
- Wishes and blessings that you hope will come true

Writing a letter like this is not just a nice thing to do; it's a meaningful way to leave something behind for the people who have been a part of your life and will continue after you have gone. It's a beautiful way to honor your relationships, share what was most important, and leave a lasting legacy.

Take time today to start writing those special notes to ensure they are found when the time comes. Remember: write letters that reflect who you are as a person, honor those closest to you, and leave behind positive lessons and advice for generations to come.

Of course, no need to write Houdini. He'll be back.

FUN THINGS TO DO

Talk:

TELL stories about those that are no longer with us, what gifts did they leave behind. TALK about how you felt when you were a kid and loss someone or something you loved. Talk about what made them special to you.

Recommend to Read:

- In Grandpaw's Pawprints by Lauren Mosback
- All Around Us by Xelena Gonzalez
- Invisible String by Patrice Karst

Questions to Ask:

What do you think is the meaning of life?

How would you celebrate someone or somethings life after they are gone?

Why do you think that people are sad after someone/something dies?

CORE VALUE: STRENGTH

Strength doesn't come from what you can do. It comes from the things you thought you couldn't.

Talk Date:

Books:

Stories:

Questions Asked:

Did You Know? 1 in 5 people have dyslexia.

What is dyslexia? It isn't just reversing letters. Dyslexia is a language-based learning difference that affects a person's ability to connect letters to sounds, making it difficult to read and spell. Reading can feel like the letters jump all over the page.

To support those with dyslexia, there are various accommodations for easier reading. One method is to use a special font. CJ Corki's books are written in the OpenDyslexic3 font to make it easier for dyslexic and non-dyslexic readers to process.

How does it work? OpenDyslexic uses "heaviness," a typography technique that increases the visual weight of a typeface which helps prevent letters from turning upside down and therefore increases one's ability to distinguish individual letters designed to reduce reading errors and the overall effort it takes to read text.

Join the learning movement for people with dyslexia at school, home, and in the community.

Meet the Authors

Meet CJ Corki, a beloved children's book author that is now venturing into the non-fiction sector. CJ Corki is three of five sisters who selected the name as a tribute to their father: CJ representing his initials, and Corki, a Polish derivative of daughters. Equipped with the magical stories from their dad, they are revealing these morsels of wit and wisdom with the rising generation.

Their goal is to inspire grandparents to share their family values and individual abilities to bridge the future generation by building memoires together.

Now, with their new non-fiction book, "Not My Monkeys: Influencing without Power," CJ is sharing their wealth of knowledge with a wider audience. This book is a collection of their hard learned experiences and stories, along with reflections on the values and life lessons they teach. With its engaging and thought-provoking writing, the book has been described as a must-read for anyone looking to deepen their understanding of what truly matters in their relationships with the grandkids.

Whenever possible, they jet-set across the country to spend weekends together—sipping wine, giving talks about the importance of intentional grandparents under the big top.